PETER DAVISON'S BOOK OF ALIEN PLANETS

It had b[illegible]ining for seven years; thousands upon t[illegible] and filled fr[illegible] the dr[illegible] crysta[illegible]f storms[illegible]e over t[illegible]n crush[illegible] a thousand [illegible]is was the way life was forever [illegible]et Venus, and this was the schoolroom of the children of the rocket men and women who had come to a raining world to set up civilization and live out their lives.

Also available in Sparrow Books

Peter Davison's Book of Alien Monsters

Peter Davison's Book of Alien Planets

SPARROW BOOKS

A Sparrow Book
Published by Arrow Books Limited
17–21 Conway Street, London W1P 6JD

An imprint of the Hutchinson Publishing Group

London Melbourne Sydney Auckland
Johannesburg and agencies throughout the world

First published 1983

Set in Linotron Baskerville
by Rowland Phototypesetting Ltd
Bury St Edmunds, Suffolk

Made and printed in Great Britain
by The Anchor Press Ltd
Tiptree, Essex

ISBN 0 09 930880 0

Contents

Introduction

by PETER DAVISON

In what might be termed the first book of the series, a book of Alien Monsters no less, I expressed my sense of honour at having such a book of my own. Well, I'm honoured again. A year has passed and as Doctor Who I have confronted a few more alien monsters and in my spare time, just to get away from it all, I have been reading about strange places in faraway galaxies. Now I find myself presenting to you a book of Alien Planets. The stories were chosen, somewhat selfishly perhaps, because I like them. I hope you do too.

Homecoming

STEPHEN DAVID

At the beginning and end of the typhoon season, when the winds were rising and falling, you could use the currents to glide between the Cities in a flitter with its small motor turned off. The favoured game was to ignore the flight decks and glide straight in at one of the portals, swooping over the galleries and terrifying the people walking there. Naturally, this was extremely dangerous. If you missed the portal, the impact with the City's hull could kill you; if it didn't, the two-kilometre drop to the ground probably would. It was a very popular game, and though it wasn't illegal to turn your motor off, it was very illegal to fly in populated areas of the Cities.

Jann had never played the Game. The idea of hurtling through the air with nothing between him and the ground was terrifying. He sometimes had nightmares of falling, hurtling down, seeing the twin Cities towering above him, then turning over in the air to see the ground and the waving heads of the tall fever trees spinning crazily beneath him. Each time, he would wake, sometimes shouting.

It was just such a dream that woke him one night. It was the middle of the season of Roaring Winds and as he lay, sweating, in his bunk, he could feel the swaying motion as the City strained against its massive mooring cables. In the bunk below him his sister Katya stirred and mumbled. Jann threw back his quilt, slipped to the ground and padded quietly into the tiny kitchen. His father was sitting quietly at the counter, watching a scientific programme on the small viewing screen. He looked up.

'Can't sleep?'

'I had the dream again,' Jann said. He climbed on to the stool next to his father's and sat, rubbing his eyes.

'The falling dream?' Jann nodded. This was the fifth time since the typhoons had started.

'Well,' his father said, 'you'd better stay up till the dream's gone. Look.' He pointed at the viewing screen. 'They're showing the lift-off simulations.' On the screen a computer image showed the City slowly revolving. Down the side of the screen a scale showed that from base to top the City was just over two kilometres high. Narrow at the base, it broadened out to the kilometre-deep cylinder that housed the living and industrial areas, then tapered again towards the top where the command centres were. Coloured arrows showed the wind direction. At first the arrows moved slowly, then gradually got faster. The City was spinning, like a top, the speed of rotation increasing as the thrust motors augmented the wind's effect. Again, the speed increased, and again, until the lines of the City were a blur. Then it was moving forwards and upwards, its rotation forcing it out to break free of the planet's weak gravity. Instead of sailing majestically a kilometre or so above the surface, harvesting the fever trees where they could, the Cities would finally break free entirely and sail where those who had built them had intended them to go: into space, into the galaxy – and home. The long exile would be over.

'When will we go?' Jann asked.

'Next typhoon season,' his father said. 'We need another half-year's good harvesting, then we'll have supplies to last us years in space.'

Jann frowned. 'Tomas didn't want us to go.'

'I think Tomas was just repeating what his parents said.'

'No,' said Jann, irritated. 'He thought a lot about it. He said we'd been here hundreds of years and no-one on Earth would remember us, and even if we got back there we wouldn't be happy. He said we should just build small ships and send a few people back to make contact. There must be lots of inhabited planets by now, and we wouldn't have to go all the way back to Earth before finding one.'

'No,' said his father with an air that Jann knew meant the discussion was over, 'there would be no point. This planet will never be a good place to live. We don't want to spend our lives trapped in these floating Cities – and even if *I* have to, there's no reason for you to. In my lifetime or yours we've got to go Home, back where we belong. And it's a long journey. On a small ship, the crew might be dead of old age before they got anywhere.'

'Well,' said Jann, 'Tomas is staying.'

'Tomas is dead, Jann,' his father said softly. 'He played the Game and he fell. No-one could survive that.'

'No,' said Jann. 'I suppose not.' He slid off the stool and went back to his bunk and a dreamless sleep.

The typhoon roared on. From the Cities to the horizon little could be seen through the clouds of reddish pollen blown by the shrieking gales. The preparations for the Return continued. In the great public halls people listened to lectures on why they were going, talks on Earth's history and culture. In the long corridors, the shopping plazas, and the cafés, they wondered: how long would it take, would any of them live to see the Homecoming? Might they roam space for decades, for hundreds of years, wandering the galaxy lost and hopeless? And if they found Earth, what would it be like? Would they be remembered – the descendants of the colonists who had disappeared hundreds of years before? Might Earth even be a dead planet, devastated by war or epidemic? On and on went the talk, round and round in circles. And in the tiny living quarters, families listened to the instructions blaring from the City's public address system and practised strapping themselves into their bunks as they would have to when the time of departure came.

Slowly the winds dropped. The quiet season came and the harvesting went on. People continued to talk. Every evening Jann would listen to his parents discussing the departure. He thought about Tomas, his friend, who would not be going.

There came a day when the winds began to rise again. Standing in the vast gallery that overlooked the space between his City, City One, and City Two, Jann could see the first flitters swoop through the early pollen clouds, wheeling and circling before dropping towards the flight decks or portals of the City. That was the way Tomas had gone. No-one had seen it happen, but he had left City One and was never seen again. His name was added to the list of victims of the Game; his family and friends mourned him; and Jann wondered. He wondered, because when it happened he had not been surprised. While some of Tomas's friends argued about whether he had smashed into the City's hull or lost control and plummeted to his death, Jann thought of the conversation he and Tomas had had only a few days before Tomas disappeared.

They had been walking along the main corridor on 'D' level, on their way home from class. As so often, they were talking about departure. At times like these, Jann always felt that Tomas might be right: he was so passionate, but also so logical. It was only when he repeated Tomas's arguments to his parents that they seemed not to work so well.

'*We'll* be foreigners,' Tomas had said. 'We've all grown up in the Cities, we only know Earth from the material in the libraries – and all of that was recorded hundreds of years ago . . .'

'But we *came* from Earth,' Jann protested. 'They must remember that a shipfull of colonists went missing. Maybe they've even been searching –' Tomas laughed, though not pleasantly.

'When someone goes down in the Game,' he said harshly, 'how long do they look for them?' He did not wait for an answer. 'These days, they don't. They assume the person's death. And they'd only have to search a few square miles to make sure, not half an interstellar space. C'mon, Jann: a ship travelling at near light speeds goes missing after passing through an asteroid belt? Who's gonna search? You assume the whole thing's dust and carry on looking for the next inhabitable planet. Shall I tell you what will happen if we turn up near a human-occupied planet?' Jann grunted, unwilling, but Tomas steamed on. 'Two massive ships – *they* won't know they're cities – appear in your segment of space, so big you could fit an Earth-type city into each of them. If we're *lucky*, they surround us and escort us out of their bit of the galaxy. If we're unlucky, they just blast us out of the space. We don't *belong* there – we belong *here*.' He gestured round. Although it looked as if he was pointing at the wide, crowded corridor, it seemed to Jann that he meant something else.

'But this planet is so hostile –' Jann began to say.

'It's not the planet,' said Tomas fiercely, 'it's *us*! We never tried. When the colony ship landed here, they took one look at the place, said "Ugh!" and started planning ways of escaping. And ever since, every effort we're capable of, all our energy, have been put towards getting away. If we'd spent all that time and cleverness in figuring out ways of staying we wouldn't be cooped up in these rusty tin cans now . . .' Jann looked around. True, parts of the City were looking a little dilapidated. The Council always said there was no time for 'minor maintenance'.

'But Tomas,' Jann said, feeling as ever slow and witless in the face of Tomas's conviction, 'everyone else seems to agree we've got to go. Surely people wouldn't go on believing something that's not true for so long?'

'*Every*one? No, not everyone. I'll tell you who doesn't agree: the harvesters don't agree. And those of us who play the Game don't agree. Now, why should that be?' The harvesters were those who used the flitters for their real purpose – gathering the pulpy fruit of the vast fever trees, which the Cities converted into almost every kind of eating and drinking material. Jann shook his head, and Tomas went on, 'Because we're the ones who go outside and look at the planet. The harvesters get right down to the surface, almost, and we at least smell the air and feel the wind on our faces. Jann, this planet is *beautiful*!'

'How can you say that? Half the year is typhoon season. The rest of the year it's just barren except for the fever trees.'

'Come and glide Jann. Come tomorrow. Then you'll understand.'

Jann shook his head. Then he said, 'Be careful Tomas. We've only one season left before we depart. Don't end up smashed to bits down there.'

Tomas gave him a curious smile. 'I won't,' he said, 'but I'm not going. And I'm not the only one.'

'But how –' Before Jann could say any more, Tomas broke away.

'If you want to know, come and play the Game tomorrow. Otherwise – well, if I happen not to be around anymore, don't worry too much . . .' Abruptly, he was gone. A few days later Jann heard that he had disappeared, was assumed dead.

He missed Tomas. Although they frequently argued, Jann felt that this left them both stronger. Tomas was unorthodox, a dreamer. Jann seemed cautious, conservative – often, it was his quiet practicality that punctured Tomas's wilder balloons such as his scheme to smuggle a flitter, piece by piece, to the very top of the City (where there was almost no atmosphere) and ride it down all the way to the flight decks. But Jann liked Tomas's challenges. Without him – and he had few other friends – he felt half-empty. And it had been a whole season now.

It happened gradually. First, he took to watching the flitters in the Game. Then, he began to sneak out at dawn to watch the dusty red sunrise. Even then a few daring youngsters would be playing the Game.

After several mornings, Jann found himself heading, as if propelled by some force outside himself, down to the flightdeck. It was a large, rectangular hangar, open to the sky at one end. Down one wall stood a row of flitters, down the other a row of large hoppers, used to carry the fever tree pulp up to the Cities. A group of youngsters was standing by a flitter at the open end of the hangar; beyond the portal the flightdeck jutted out, a narrow platform hanging over the void. As Jann slowly approached the group, a black-painted flitter swooped noiselessly down. Its skis slid smoothly on the flightdeck, the flitter's wings folding back as it swept into the hangar. It came to a halt by the waiting group. The hood slid back and a girl stepped out. About Jann's age, she had long black hair and a fierce-looking face. He recognized her as a girl from City Two called Keri. Tomas had spoken admiringly of her. There was a burst of applause from the group. Then one of them, a boy Jann didn't know, broke away and took Keri's place in the flitter. The motor hummed into life, and within seconds the flitter was speeding down the flight deck. As soon as it was clear, its motor would be switched off.

Keri ignored the group and set off down the hangar. As she neared Jann he stepped in front of her, blocking her way. She stopped.

'Tomas said you'd come in the end,' she said.

'What did he mean?'

'About what?'

'About staying here. And not being the only one.'

'Why don't you ask him?'

'How can I?' Jann was fast getting furious. 'He's dead!'

'If you think that,' she said slowly and emphatically, gazing for the first time into his eyes, '*Why are you here*?' Furiously, he grabbed her arm, but she pulled away and set off down the hangar. He followed her.

'Every question I ask, you ask me one back. I'm his friend. *Where is he*?'

She did not break her stride. 'Are your family going?' she asked.

He was bewildered. 'Going? Of course. Everyone is.'

'Tomas isn't.'

'But he's –' A terrible thought struck Jann for the first time. 'You mean he's alive . . . down there, on the surface?' She didn't answer. 'But if he is then they ought to send a rescue party, get him back. He'll *die*. Maybe he's hurt. And the fever trees . . . he'll get the fever . . .' His voice had risen and he was suddenly aware that he was shrieking.

At last she stopped. 'All right,' she said, 'have you

been to see Tomas's parents?' Shamefaced, Jann admitted he had not. 'Fine.' Keri said, 'then we'll go to see them. You can tell them what you think.' Helplessly, he trailed in her wake.

Jann was shocked when Keri did not bother to press the buzzer of the apartment, more shocked when she coolly pressed the code combination to let them in, and astounded when they found the place empty. There was nothing to show that Tomas or his parents had ever been there. None of the little personal possessions that people used to differentiate the otherwise identical living quarters. It was incomprehensible. If the family were dead, the quarters would be occupied by new people by now – the public dormitories were hugely overcrowded and there were long waiting lists for the private apartments. That this apartment was empty could only mean that no-one knew the family were gone. Except Keri. And himself. Abruptly he sat on the floor, leant back against a bare wall.

'Where are they?' Keri stood in the middle of the room, arms folded, looking down at him, a faint smile on her face.

'With Tomas,' she said.

'Are they hiding?'

'In a way.'

'In City Two?'

'There's only one way to find out, Jann. Play the Game. That's what Tomas told you, wasn't it?'

'But if he's in Two, there's no need – we can just go over on the ferry.'

'Jann, it's a matter of *trust.*' Keri knelt down, her voice low. 'Tomas wanted you to come out with us, he wanted to tell you . . . what was happening. But you wouldn't come, so he wasn't allowed to say anything. He still wants to talk to you, but you've got to give something in return. You've got to make the trip. Then he'll tell you everything.'

Jann knew well enough how to do it. He'd spent many hours in the huge freefall chambers at the top of the City, piloting a flitter in the artificial winds, secure in the knowledge that if anything went wrong an automatic safety device would immediately land machine and pilot softly and safely. This, though, would not be recreation. He thought of his dream. Keri was watching him closely.

'If you don't,' she said, 'you'll never see Tomas again.' Weakly he nodded, feeling sick and afraid.

Somehow, when they got back to the hangar, the portal at the far end seemed menacing, and Jann fancied he could see the unpredictable winds gusting past. He thought of the emptiness below the flightdeck and shuddered. Keri pointed him towards a flitter.

'I'll keep beside you,' she said. 'Mostly, once we're out there we open the hoods. The air's thin but breathable. You don't have to, but I'd recommend it. What you *do* have to do is switch the motor off.'

He slipped into the cockpit, slid the hood shut and started the motor. He did everything quickly because he was scared and did not want to think. As the flitter slid gently along the hangar towards the flightdeck he realized he'd forgotten to let the wings swing shut. He pressed the button. He was dimly aware of Keri's flitter to his right. Then they were out of the hangar and on the flightdeck and he gasped. All around him was light, bright and shadowy, dappled with clouds of moisture and pollen. In the distance City Two revolved slowly, magnificently, its hull plates sparkling in the light. Suddenly Jann realized the flitter was in the air, had left the flightdeck. Forgetting to be afraid he cut the motor. And opened the hood.

The air was warm. There was a smell, something Jann couldn't identify: somehow it made him feel hungry, it was rich and appetising but like nothing he had smelled in the City. And the colours: from a rich indigo above him, so blue and deep he felt he could lose himself in it, to a pale translucent blue in the distance ahead of him. He looked over to Keri's flitter and, suddenly joyous, waved. He saw her grin, then she waved her hand and pointed downwards. The nose of her flitter dipped. Suddenly alarmed, Jann kept his flitter on an even course, constantly adjusting as the winds gusted around him. He lost sight of Keri and wondered where she had gone. Ahead he could see City Two's flightdeck, now only a matter of minutes away. It hadn't been so bad. He would talk to Tomas then get the ferry back.

Above and to his left there was an angry buzzing. Startled he looked up and there, hovering dangerously close – *and with its motor on* – was Keri's flitter. His brain screamed at him to evade her, but before his hands could obey, she had dropped to her right. Her wing hit his and, with a lurch, his flitter dropped. Frantically Jann fought to get the little craft back on an even keel. After what seemed hours, it levelled off. Sweating, he looked round. No sign of Keri, and he still had the height to make it to the flightdeck. And now he knew. Whatever was going on, he had been told too much. Keri had tried to kill him.

She attacked again, just as his finger was poised over the button to start the motor. Again the wings met and Jann's craft lurched sickeningly downwards. Again, he fought to regain control, not daring to start the motor until he was flying level. And then he had it, the nose straightened, and he pressed the starter button. Nothing happened. He pressed it again. Nothing. And he was now too low to make the flightdeck.

Keri appeared at his right again. He glared at her.

To his astonishment she smiled and made an unmistakable 'follow me' sign. Swiftly, he considered the alternatives. Keri banked steeply to the right and began a long, slow spiral down. Mentally shrugging, Jann followed.

His flitter passed within metres of City Two. This far down there were no observation posts, just ventilation ducts, sluices, inspection hatches. Above, he could see the vast outlets of the thrust motors, the hull beneath them blackened. Then he was below the City looking up. He felt dizzy at the sight of two kilometres of towering metal looming over him. He began to feel that it was about to fall on top of him, and hastily looked down. For the first time in his life, Jann saw a landscape without a city floating above it. He was now only a thousand metres up and could see below him a large patch of fever trees. Beyond them was a flat expanse of something that glinted, from which a silver ribbon wound across the flat, reddish landscape. There was no sound except for the rush of wind. Spiralling below him, he could see Keri's flitter.

Only a minute later they were below the level of the fever trees, whose odd, bulbous shapes strangely echoed the shapes of the Cities that floated above them. Below the bulbous plants sprouted the sharp leaves, metres across, that gave the trees their name.

Between the plants and the strange, glinting area, was an expanse of flat ground and it was here that Keri landed. Jann brought his flitter in behind her. As he did so, his pleasure in the glide down evaporated in a burst of anger at what she had done. As soon as his flitter had halted he leapt from the cockpit and ran furiously towards her. Keri, standing by her flitter, kept her ground and, as he approached, pointed behind him. Something in her face stopped him, and he turned. There, standing at the edge of the grove of fever trees, was Tomas, and his parents.

It was quiet and peaceful in the shade of the trees. The leaves rose for some metres, leaving enough space beneath them for the small settlement of huts constructed from the fibre of the trees. In the foliage above small creatures chittered comfortably, clicking their tongues in a dozy, muttering way. Beyond the edge of the grove, past the two flitters, water lapped gently on the stony shore, reflecting the starlight. There was a soft murmur of voices as people talked after the evening meal. Jann was sitting with Keri, and with Tomas and his parents outside their hut.

'I told you,' Tomas said, but this time there was no anger in his voice, 'we're not going. This is our home.' He pointed at the lake. 'Until today, you had no idea that lakes even existed. Let me tell you: swimming in water is as much fun as flitting. *And* you can drink it. *And* there are fish there to eat.' They had just eaten fish. Jann had never tasted anything so wonderful. He was bemused – not at what he was seeing, but that so few people in the Cities understood.

'I thought it was all hostile,' he said, 'and the leaves of the plants, and the pollen – people *died*.'

'At first,' said Tomas's father. 'People who touched the leaves got fever and died after terrible hallucinations. But we soon became resistant: it's been hundreds of years since a death. But people weren't willing to try. They'd left Earth in a colony ship because Earth was so overcrowded it was choking to death. They were full of dreams, obsessed with finding a fresh planet, one where clear streams ran through green meadows and high mountains sparkled against a clear blue sky. But one ship, carrying a thousand colonists, had an accident. An asteroid damaged it so badly it lost contact with the others and had to seek refuge on the nearest planet.' He paused. 'Here. And what did they find? Lots of stony ground and the fever trees. Within days there were deaths. They stayed in the ship, trying to repair it – and failed. They were stuck on a planet that was the opposite of all they had hoped for.'

The groups of people around the huts had fallen silent, listening now. They must all know the story, Jann thought, but they need to hear it again.

'It was hard at first, just surviving. But in the ship they had all they needed to make the most of any planet they were on. They had mining equipment, laboratories, computerized factories, flitters, you name it. The one thing they didn't have was the capacity to build a new fusion plant to get them off the planet.

'Now, the idea was that when they landed, they'd build a town and start making the planet a good place to live. But what our ancestors did instead was to bed down in the disabled colony ship and start figuring out ways to get away.

'They'd only been here a month or so when the typhoon season started. They weren't ready for it, so that halved the population. But when it was all over, one of them remembered something he'd seen . . .' Tomas's father paused dramatically and gestured upwards. 'As the winds built up the fever trees began spinning. And just when the typhoon started they spun so hard they took off into the sky, flinging pollen every which way.'

'So there *is* a reason why the shapes look the same,' Jann exclaimed.

'It's the same principle. The planet's got low gravity and that typhoon can act like a whip on a spinning top. Mind you, it took hundreds of years. The first cities were top heavy. They crashed. It was only about four generations ago that One and Two finally became habitable. And in all those hundreds of years, we learned so little about this planet. Oh, we learned to harvest the pulp from the trees. But then we got into the Cities and most of us turned our backs on the outside world. Most people up there aren't capable even of thinking that living down here is possible. And in a few days . . .'

'They'll leave without you,' Jann broke in. Around him, the family smiled. Tomas gestured at the group of huts, the people sitting quietly at their doorways in the warm air, the soft murmur of conversation.

'Yes,' he said quietly, 'but they're leaving us in our home. Jann, people have been slipping away from the Cities for some time now. We aren't the only settlement. We know this plant isn't Paradise: but there *is* enough to eat and we *will* survive and, in the end, we will cultivate it and build towns and, one day, even cities.'

'But even if we fail,' said Keri, 'at least we'll do it here, not wandering the galaxy trying to get back to the very thing we fled from.'

'Jann, stay with us,' said Tomas. Jann looked around him. Starlight softly illuminated the quiet clearing. Above them, the giant fever trees swayed. Warm air carried the smell of the water that sparkled beyond the trees. He sighed.

The next morning Jann climbed into the flitter. Keri had repaired her sabotage of the motor. He settled in the seat and looked down at Tomas and Keri.

'I've got to go,' he said. 'All my life I've lived with the dream of all of us going back into space and finding the rest of the human race. There must be lots of planets by now with people on them. We seem so – cut off here. Nothing's happened here, ever.'

'Jann,' said Tomas gently, 'that's because the people who wanted to leave wouldn't *let* anything happen.'

'Well,' said Jann, 'yes, but I must go. I like your world, but I must go.'

'And I thought *I* was the dreamer,' said Tomas.

Jann laughed. 'I'll come back,' he said, 'and by then there'll be a nice big town here, and you'll be mayor.'

'He won't,' said Keri, 'I will.'

The little flitter climbed up, over the fever trees and towards the great Cities poised in the sky. City One loomed closer and closer. Deftly, Jann piloted the flitter onto the flightdeck and taxied into the hangar. He was home.

Below, Tomas and Keri gazed up. The waves on the lake were getting higher, whipped up by the gathering winds. Dust was blowing and pollen from the trees filled the air. There was a creaking noise from the great trunks of the fever trees.

Above them, the two shining cities began to revolve more quickly.

Grenville's Planet

MICHAEL SHAARA

Wisher did not see the brightness because he was back aft alone. In the still ship he sat quietly, relaxed. He was not bored. It was just that he had no interest. After fourteen years in the Mapping Command even the strangest of the new worlds was routine to him and what little imagination he had was beginning to centre upon a small farm he had seen on the southern plains of Vega VII.

The brightness that Wisher did not see grew with the passing moments. A pale young man named Grenville, who was Wisher's crewman, watched it for a long while absently. When the gleam took on brilliance and a blue-white, dazzling blaze Grenville was startled. He stared at the screen for a long moment, then carefully checked the distance. Still a few light minutes away, the planet was already uncommonly bright.

Pleasantly excited, Grenville watched the planet grow. Slowly the moons came out. Four winked on and ringed the bright world like pearls in a necklace. Grenville gazed in awe. The blueness and the brightness flowed in together, it was the most beautiful thing that Grenville had ever seen.

Excited, he buzzed for Wisher. Wisher did not come.

Grenville took the ship in close and now it occurred to him to wonder. That a planet should shine like that, like an enormous facet of polished glass, was incredible. Now, as he watched, the light began to form vaguely into the folds of cloud. The blue grew richer and deeper. Long before he hit the first cloud layer, Grenville knew what it was. He pounded the buzzer. Wisher finally came.

When he saw the water in the screen he stopped in his tracks.

'Well I'll be damned!' he breathed.

Except for a few scuds of clouds it was blue. The entire world was blue. There was the white of the clouds and the icecaps, but the rest was all blue and the rest was water.

Grenville began to grin. A world of *water*!

'Now how's *that* for a freak?' he chuckled. 'One in a million, right, Sam? I bet you never saw anything like that.'

Wisher shook his head, still staring. Then he moved quickly to the controls and set out to make a check. They circled the planet with the slow, spiralling motion of the Mapping Command, bouncing radar off the dark side. When they came back into the daylight they were sure. There was no land on the planet.

Grenville, as usual, began to chatter.

'Well, naturally,' he said, 'it was bound to happen sooner or later. Considering Earth, which has a land area covering only one fourth –'

'Yep,' nodded Wisher.

'– and when you consider the odds, chances are that there are quite a number of planets with scarcely any land area at all.'

Wisher had moved back to the screen.

'Let's go down,' he said.

Grenville, startled, stared at him.

'Where?'

'Down low, I want to see what's living in that ocean.'

Because each new world was a wholly *new* world and because experience therefore meant nothing, Wisher had decided a long while ago to follow the regs without question. For without the regs, the Mapping Command was a death trap. Nowhere in space was the need for rules so great as out on the frontier where there were no rules at all. The regs were complex, efficient and all-embracing; it was to the regs that the men of the Mapping Command owed their lives and the rest of Mankind owed the conquest of space.

But inevitably, unalterably, there were things which the regs could not have foreseen. And Wisher knew that too, but he did not think about it.

According to plan, then, they dropped down into the stratosphere, went further down below the main cloud region and levelled off at a thousand feet. Below them, mile after rolling, billowy mile, the sea flowed out to the great bare circle of the horizon.

With the screen at full magnification, they probed the water.

It was surprising, in all that expanse of sea, to observe so little. No schools of fish of any kind, no floating masses of seaweed, nothing but a small fleet shape here and there and an occasional group of tiny plant organisms.

Wisher dropped only a hundred or so feet lower. In a world where evolution had been confined underwater it would be best to keep at a distance. On the other worlds to which he had come Wisher had seen some vast and incredible things. Eight hundred feet up, he thought, is a good safe distance.

It was from that height then, that they saw the island.

It was small, too small to be seen from a distance, was barely five miles in length and less than two miles wide. A little brown cigar it was, sitting alone in the varying green-blue wash of the ocean.

Grenville began to grin. Abruptly he laughed out loud. Grenville was not the kind of man who is easily awed, and the sight of that one bare speck, that single stubby persistent butt of rock alone in a world of water, was infinitely comical to him.

'Wait'll we show the boys *this*,' he chuckled to Wisher. 'Break out the camera. My God, what a picture *this* will make!'

Grenville was filled with pride. This planet, after all, was *his* assignment. It was his to report on, his discovery – he gasped. They might even name it after *him*.

He flushed, his heart beat rapidly. It had happened before. There were a number of odd planets named after men in the Mapping Command. When the tourists came they would be coming to Grenville's Planet, one of the most spectacular wonders of the Universe.

While the young man was thus rejoicing, Wisher had brought the ship around and was swinging slowly in over the island. It was covered with some kind of brownish-green, stringy vegetation. Wisher was tempted to go down and check for animal life, but decided to see first if there were any more islands.

Still at a height of 800 feet, they spiralled the planet. They did not see the second island, radar picked it out for them.

This one was bigger than the first and there was another island quite near to the south. Both were narrow and elongated in the cigar-like shape of the first, were perhaps twenty miles in length and were encrusted with the same brown-green vegetation. They were small enough to have been hidden from sight during the first check by a few scattered clouds.

The discovery of them was anticlimactic and disappointing. Grenville would have been happier if there was no land at all. But he regained some of his earlier enthusiasm when he remembered that the tourists would still come and that now at least they would be able to land.

There was nothing at all on the night side. Coming back out into the daylight, Wisher cautiously decided to take them down.

'Peculiar,' said Wisher, peering at the dunes of the beach.

'What is?' Grenville eyed him through the fish bowls of their helmets.

'I don't know,' Wisher turned slowly, gazed around at the shaggy, weedy vegetation. 'It doesn't feel right.'

Grenville fell silent. There was nothing on the island that could hurt them, they were quite sure of that. The check had revealed the presence of a great number of small, four-footed animals, but only one type was larger than a dog, and that one was slow and noisy.

'Have to be careful about snakes,' Wisher said absently, recalling the regs on snakes and insects. Funny thing, that. There were very few insects.

Both men were standing in close to the ship. It was the rule, of course. You never left the ship until you were absolutely sure. Wisher, for some vague reason he could not define, was not sure.

'How's the air check?'

Grenville was just then reading the meters. After a moment he said, 'Good.'

Wisher relaxed, threw open his helmet and breathed in deeply. The clean fresh air flowed into him, exhilarating him. He unscrewed his helmet entirely, looking around.

The ship had come down on the up end of the beach, a good distance from the sea, and was standing now in a soft, reddish sand. It was bordered on the north by the open sea and to the south was the scrawny growth they had seen from above. It was not a jungle – the plants were too straight and stiff for that – and the height of the tallest was less than ten feet. But it was the very straightness of things, the eerie regularity of them, which grated in Wisher's mind.

But, breathing in the cool sea air of the island, Wisher began to feel more confident. They had their rifles, they had the ship and the alarm system. There was nothing here that could harm them.

Grenville brought out some folding chairs from the ship. They sat and chatted pleasantly until the twilight came.

Just before twilight two of the moons came out.

'Moons,' said Wisher suddenly.

'What.'

'I was just thinking,' Wisher explained.

'What about the moons?'

'I wasn't thinking exactly about them, I was thinking about the tide. Four good-sized moons in conjunction could raise one heck of a tide.'

Grenville settled back, closing his eyes.

'So?'

'So that's probably where the land went.'

Grenville was too busy dreaming about his fame as discoverer of Grenville's Planet to be concerned with tides and moons.

'Let the techs worry about that,' he said without interest.

But Wisher kept thinking.

The tide could very well be the cause. When the four moons got together and started to pull they would raise a tremendous mass of water, a grinding power that would slice away the continent edges like no erosive force in history. Given a billion years in which to work – but Wisher suddenly remembered a peculiar thing about the island.

If the tides had planed down the continents of this planet, then these islands had no right being here, certainly not as sand and loose rock. Just one tide like the ones those moons could raise would be enough to cut the islands completely away. Well maybe, he thought, the tides are very far apart, centuries even.

He glanced apprehensively at the sky. The two moons visible were reassuringly far apart.

He turned from the moons to gaze at the sea. And then he remembered the first thought he had had about this planet – that uncomfortable feeling that the first sight of land had dispelled. He thought of it now again.

Evolution.

A billion years beneath the sea, with no land to take the first developing mammals. What was going on, right now, as he watched, beneath the placid rolling surface of the sea?

It was a disturbing thought. When they went back to the ship for the night Wisher did not need the regs to tell him to seal the airlock and set the alarm screens.

The alarm that came in the middle of the night and nearly scared Wisher to death turned out to be only an animal. It was one of the large ones, a weird bristling thing with a lean and powerful body. It got away before they were up to see it, but it left its photographic image.

In spite of himself, Wisher had trouble getting back to sleep, and in the morning was silently in favour of leaving for the one last star they would map before returning to base. But the regs called for life specimens to be brought back from all livable worlds whenever possible, whenever there was no 'slight manifestation of danger'. Well, here it was certainly possible. They would have to stay long enough to take a quick sampling of plants and animals and of marine life too.

Grenville was just as anxious to get back as Wisher was, but for different reasons. Grenville, figured Grenville, was now a famous man.

Early in the morning, then, they lifted ship and once more spiralled the planet. Once the mapping radar had recorded the size and shape and location of the islands, they went in low again and made a complete check for life forms.

They found as before, very little. There were the bristling things, and – as Wisher had suspected – a great quantity of snakes and lizards. There were very few observable fish. There were no birds.

When they were done they returned to the original island. Grenville, by this time, had a name for it. Since there was another island near it, lying to the south, Grenville called that one South Grenville. The first was, of course, North Grenville. Grenville chuckled over that for a long while.

'Don't go too near the water.'

'All right, mama,' Grenville chirped, grinning. 'I'll work the edge of the vegetation.'

'Leave the rifle, take the pistol. It's handier.'

Grenville nodded and left, dragging the specimen sack. Wisher, muttering, turned toward the water.

It is unnatural, he thought, for a vast warm ocean to be so empty of life. Because the ocean, really, is where life begins. He had visions in his mind of any number of vicious, incredible, slimy things that were alive and native to that sea and who were responsible for the unnatural sterility of the water. When he approached the waves he was very cautious.

The first thing he noticed, with a shock, was that there were no shellfish.

Not any. Not crabs or snails or even the tiniest of sea beings. Nothing. The beach was a bare, dead plot of sand.

He stood a few yards from the waves, motionless. He was almost positive, now, that there was danger here. The shores of every warm sea he had ever seen, from Earth on out to Deneb, had been absolutely choked with life and the remnants of life. There were always shells and fish scales, and snails, worms, insects; bits of jellyfish, tentacles, minutiae of a hundred million kinds, cluttering and crowding every square inch of the beach and sea. And yet here, now, there was nothing. Just sand and water.

It took a great deal of courage for Wisher to approach those waves, although the water here was shallow. He took a quick water sample and hurried back to the ship.

Minutes later he was perched in the shadow of her side, staring out broodingly over the ocean. The water was Earth water as far as his instruments could tell. There was nothing wrong with it. But there was nothing much living in it.

When Grenville came back with the floral specimens Wisher quietly mentioned the lack of shellfish.

'Well, hell,' said Grenville, scratching his head painfully, 'maybe they just don't like it here.'

And maybe they've got reason, Wisher said to himself. But aloud he said, 'The computer finished calculating the orbits of those moons.'

'So?'

'So the moons conjunct every 112 years. They raise a tide of 600 feet.'

Grenville did not follow.

'The tide,' said Wisher, smiling queerly, 'is at least 400 feet higher than any of the islands.'

When Grenville started, still puzzled, Wisher grunted and kicked at the sand.

'Now where in hell do you suppose the animals came from?'

'They should be drowned,' said Grenville slowly.

'Right. And would be, unless they're amphibian, which they're not. Or unless a new batch evolves every hundred years.'

'Um,' Grenville sat down to think about it.

'Don't make sense,' he said after a while.

Having thoroughly confounded Grenville, Wisher turned away and paced slowly in the sand. The sand, he thought distractedly, that's another thing. Why in heck is this island here at all?

Artificial.

The word popped unbidden into his brain.

That would be it. That would have to be it.

The island was artificial, was – restored. Put here by whoever or whatever lived under the sea.

Grenville was ready to go. He stood nervously eyeing the waves, his fingers clamped tightly on the pistol at his belt, waiting for Wisher to give the word.

Wisher leaned against the spaceship, conveniently near the airlock. He regretted disturbing Grenville.

'We can't leave yet,' he said calmly. 'We haven't any proof. And besides, there hasn't been any "manifestation of danger".'

'We have proof enough for me,' Grenville said quickly.

Wisher nodded absently.

'It's easy to understand. Evolution kept right on going, adapting and changing just as it does everywhere else in the Universe. Only here, when the mammals began coming up onto the land, they had no room to expand. And they were all being washed away every hundred years, as the tides rose and fell and the continents wore down below tide level.

'But evolution never stopped. It continued beneath the sea. Eventually it came up with an intelligent race.

'God knows what they are, or how far they've progressed. They must be pretty highly evolved, or they couldn't have done something like this –' he broke off, realizing that the building of the islands was no clue. The ancient Egyptians on Earth had built the pyramids, certainly a much harder job. There was no way of telling how far evolved this race was. Or what the island was for.

Zoo?

No. He shook that out of the confusion of his mind. If the things in the sea wanted a zoo they would naturally build it below the surface of the water, where they themselves could travel with ease and where the animals could be kept in airtight compartments. And if this was a zoo, then by now there should have been visitors.

That was one more perplexing thing. Why had nothing come? It was unbelievable that an island like this should be left completely alone, that nothing had noticed the coming of their ship.

And here his thought broke again. They would not be just fish, these things. They would need . . . hands. Or tentacles. He pictured something like a genius squid, and the hair on his body stiffened.

He turned back to Grenville.

'Did you get the animal specimens?'

Grenville shook his head. 'No. Just plants. And a small lizard.'

Wisher's face, lined with the inbred caution of many years, now at last betrayed his agitation. 'We'll have to get one of those things that set off the alarm last night. But to heck with the rest. We'll let HQ worry about that.' He stepped quickly into the airlock, dragging the bag of specimens. 'I'll pack up,' he said, 'you go get that thing.'

Grenville turned automatically and struck off down the beach.

He never came back.

At the end of the third hour after Grenville had gone, Wisher went to the arms locker and pulled out a heavy rifle. He cursed the fact that he had no small scout sled. He could not take the ship. She was too big and unwieldly for low, slow flying and he could not risk cracking her up.

He was breaking the regs, of course. Since Grenville had not come back he must be considered dead and it was up to Wisher to leave alone. A special force would come back for Grenville, or for what was left of him. Wisher knew all that. He thought about it while he was loading the rifle. He thought about the vow he had made never to break the regs and he went right on loading the rifle. He told himself that he would take no chances and if he didn't find Grenville right away he would come back and leave, but he knew all along that he was breaking the regs. At the same time he knew that there was nothing else to do. This was the one reg he had never faced before and it was the one reg he would always break. For Grenville or for anyone else. For a skinny young fool like Grenville, or for anyone else.

Before he left he took the routine precautions concerning the ship. He set the alarm screens to blast anything that moved within two hundred feet of her. If Grenville came back before him it would be all right because the alarm was set to deactivate when it registered the sound pattern of either his or Grenville's voice. If Grenville came back and didn't see him, he would know that the alarm was on.

And if no one came back at all, the ship would blow by itself.

The beach was wide and curved on out of sight. Grenville's deep heel prints were easy to follow.

Stiffly, in the wind, the stalks of the brown vegetation scratched and rustled. Wisher walked along Grenville's track. He wanted to call, but stopped himself. No noise. He must make no noise.

This is the end of it, he kept saying to himself. When I get out of this I will go home.

The heel prints turned abruptly into the alien forest. Wisher walked some distance farther on, to a relatively clear space. He turned, stepping carefully, started to circle the spot where Grenville had gone in. The wood around him was soggy, sterile. He saw nothing move. But a sharp, shattering blast came suddenly to him in the still air.

The explosion blossomed and Wisher perked spasmodically. The ship. Something was at the ship. He fought down a horrible impulse to run, stood quiet, gun poised, knowing that the ship could take care of itself. And then he stepped slowly forward. And fell.

He fell through a soft light mat of bushes into a hole. There was a crunching snap and he felt a metal rip into his legs, tearing and cracking the bones. He went up to his shoulders. He knew in a flash, with a blast of glacial fear, what it was. *Animal trap.*

He reached for his rifle. But the rifle was beyond him. A foot past his hand, it lay on the floor of the wood near him. His legs, his legs . . . he felt the awful pain as he tried to move.

It blazed through his mind and woke him. Out of his belt he dragged his pistol, and in a sea of pain, held upright by the trap, he waited. He was not afraid. He had broken the regs, and this had happened, and he had expected it. He waited.

Nothing came.

Why, Why?

This had happened to Grenville, he knew. Why?

It had happened to him now, and for a moment he could not understand why he did not seem to care, but was just . . . curious. Then he looked down into the hole and saw the hot redness of his own blood, and as he watched it bubble he realized that he was dying.

He had very little time. He was hopeful. Maybe something would come and at least he would see what they were. He wanted awfully for something to come. In the red mist which was his mind he debated with himself whether or not to shoot it if it came, and over and over he asked himself why, why? Before something came, unfortunately, he died.

The traps had been dug in the night. From out of the sea they had come to dig in the preserve – for a preserve was what the island was, was all that it could have been – and then returned to the sea to wait.

For the ship had been seen from the very beginning, and its purpose understood. The best brains of the sea had gathered and planned, the enormous, manta-like people whose name was unpronounceable but whose technology was not far behind Earth's, met in consultation and immediately understood. It was necessary to capture the ship. Therefore the Earthmen must be separated from it, and it was for this reason that Wisher had died.

But now, to the astonishment of the things, the ship was still alive. It stood silent and alone in the whiteness of the beach ticking and sparking within itself, and near it, on the bloodied sand, were the remains of the one that had come too close. The others had fled in terror.

Time was of no importance to the clever, squid-like beings. They had won already, could wait and consider. Thus the day grew late and became afternoon, and the waves – the aseptic, sterile waves which were proof in themselves of the greatest of all oceanic civilizations – crumbled whitely on the beach. The things exulted. The conquest of space was in their hands.

Within the ship, of course, there was ticking, and a small red hand moved toward zero.

In a little while the ship would blow, and with it would go the island, and a great chunk of the sea. But the beings could not know. It was an alien fact they faced and an alien fact was unknowable. Just as Wisher could not have known the nature of the planet, these things could not now foresee the nature of the ship and the wheel had come full circle. Second by second, with the utter, mechanical loyalty of the machine, the small red hand crept onward.

The waves near the beach were frothy and white.

A crowd was forming.

Exile

EDMOND HAMILTON

I wish now that we hadn't got to talking about science fiction that night! If we hadn't, I wouldn't be haunted now by that queer, impossible story which can't ever be proved or disproved.

But the four of us were all professional writers of fantastic stories, and I suppose shop talk was inevitable. Yet, we'd kept off it through dinner and the drinks afterwards. Madison had outlined his hunting trip with gusto, and then Brazell started a discussion of the Dodgers' chances. And then I had to turn the conversation to fantasy.

I didn't mean to do it. But I'd had an extra Scotch, and that always makes me feel analytical. And I got to feeling amused by the perfect way in which we four resembled a quartet of normal, ordinary people.

'Protective coloration, that's what it is,' I announced. 'How hard we work at the business of acting like ordinary good guys!'

Brazell looked at me, somewhat annoyed by the interruption. 'What are you talking about?'

'About us,' I answered. 'What a wonderful imitation of solid, satisfied citizens we put up! But we're not satisfied, you know – none of us. We're violently dissatisfied with the Earth, and all its works, and that's why we spend our lives dreaming up one imaginary world after another.'

'I suppose the little matter of getting paid for it has nothing to do with it?' Brazell asked sceptically.

'Sure it has,' I admitted. 'But we all dreamed up our impossible worlds and peoples long before we ever wrote a line, didn't we? From back in childhood, even? It's because we don't feel at home here.'

Madison snorted. 'We'd feel a lot less at home on some of the worlds we write about.'

Then Carrick, the fourth of our party, broke into the conversation. He'd been sitting over his drink in his usual silent way, brooding, paying no attention to us.

He was a queer chap, in most ways. We didn't know him very well, but we liked him and admired his stories. He'd done some wonderful tales of an imaginary planet – all carefully worked out.

He told Madison, 'That happened to me.'

'What happened to you?' Madison asked.

'What you were suggesting – *I* once wrote about an imaginary world and then had to live on it,' Carrick answered.

Madison laughed. 'I hope it was a more livable place than the lurid planets on which I set my own yarns.'

But Carrick was unsmiling. He murmured, 'I'd have made it a lot different – if I'd known I was ever going to live on it.'

Brazell, with a significant glance at Carrick's empty glass winked at us and then asked blandly, 'Let's hear about it, Carrick.'

Carrick kept looking dully down at his empty glass, turning it slowly in his fingers as he talked. He paused every few words.

'It happened just after I'd moved next to the big power station. It sounds like a noisy place, but actually it was very quiet out there on the edge of the city. And I had to have quiet, if I was to produce stories.

'I got right to work on a new series I was starting, the stories of which were all to be laid on the same imaginary world. I began by working out the detailed physical appearance of that world, as well as the universe that was its background. I spent the whole day concentrating on that. And, as I finished, something in my mind went *click*!

'That queer, brief mental sensation felt oddly like a sudden *crystallization*. I stood there, wondering if I were going crazy. For I had a sudden strong conviction that it meant that the universe and world I had been dreaming up all day had suddenly crystallized into physical existence somewhere.

'Naturally, I brushed aside the eerie thought and went out and forgot about it. But the next day, the thing happened again. I had spent most of that second day working up the inhabitants of my story world. I'd made them definitely human, but had decided against making them too civilized – for that would exclude the conflict and violence that must form my story.

'So, I'd made my imaginary world a world whose people were still only half-civilized. I figured out all their cruelties and superstitions. I mentally built up their colourful barbaric cities. And just as I was through – that *click*! echoed sharply in my mind.

'It startled me badly, this second time. For now I felt more strongly than before that queer conviction that my day's dreaming had crystallized into solid reality. I knew it was insane to think that, yet it was an incredible certainty in my mind. I couldn't get rid of it.

'I tried to reason the thing out so that I could dismiss that crazy conviction. If my imagining a world and universe had actually created them, where were they? Certainly not in my own cosmos. It couldn't hold two universes – each completely different from the other.

'But maybe that world and universe of my imagining had crystallized into reality in another and empty cosmos? A cosmos lying in a different dimension from my own? One which had contained only free atoms, formless matter that had not taken on shape until my concentrated thought had somehow stirred it into the forms I dreamed?

'I reasoned along like that, in the queer, dreamlike way in which you apply the rules of logic to impossibilities. How did it come that my imaginings had never crystallized into reality before, but had only just begun to do so? Well, there was a plausible explanation for that. It was the big power station nearby. Some unfathomable freak of energy radiated from it was focusing my concentrated imaginings, as super-amplified force, upon an empty cosmos where they stirred formless matter into the shapes I dreamed.

'Did I believe that? No, I didn't believe it – but I knew it. There is quite a difference between knowledge and belief, as someone said who once pointed out that all men know they will die and none of them believe it. It was like that with me. I realized it was not possible that my imaginary world had come into physical being in a different dimensional cosmos, yet at the same time I was strangely convinced that it had.

'A thought occurred to me that amused and interested me. What if I imagined *myself* in that other world? Would I, too, become physically real in it? I tried it. I sat at my desk, imagining myself as one of the millions of persons in that imaginary world, dreaming up a whole soberly realistic background and family and history for myself over there. And my mind said *click*!'

Carrick paused, still looking down at the empty glass that he twirled slowly between his fingers.

Madison prompted him. 'And of course you woke up there, and a beautiful girl was leaning over you, and you asked, "Where am I?"'

'It wasn't like that,' Carrick said dully. 'It wasn't like that at all. I woke up in that other world, yes. But it wasn't like a real awakening. I was just suddenly in it.

'I was still myself. But I was the myself I had imagined in that other world. That other me had always lived in it – and so had his ancestors before him. I had worked all that out, you see.

'And I was just as real to myself, in that imaginary world I had created, as I had been in my own. That was the worst part of it. Everything in that half-civilized world was so utterly, common-placely real.'

He paused again. 'It was queer, at first. I walked out into the streets of those barbaric cities, and looked into the people's faces, and I felt like shouting aloud, "I imagined you all! You had no existence until I dreamed of you!"

'But I didn't do that. They wouldn't have believed me. To them, I was just an insignificant single member of their race. How could they guess that they and their traditions of long history, their world and their universe, had all been suddenly brought into being by my imagination?

'After my first excitement ebbed, I didn't like the place. I had made it too barbaric. The savage violences and cruelties that had seemed so attractive as material for a story, were ugly and repulsive at first hand. I wanted nothing but to get back to my own world.

'And I couldn't get back! There just wasn't any way. I had had a vague idea that I could imagine myself back into my own world as I had imagined myself into this other one. But it didn't work that way. The freak force that had wrought the miracle didn't work two ways.

'I had a pretty bad time when I realized that I was trapped in that ugly, squalid, barbarian world. I felt like killing myself at first. But I didn't. A man can adapt himself to anything. I adapted myself the best I could to the world I had created.'

'What did you do there? What was your position, I mean?' Brazell asked.

Carrick shrugged. 'I don't know the crafts or skills of that world I'd brought into being. I had only my own skill – that of story telling.'

I began to grin. 'You don't mean to say that you started writing fantastic stories?'

He nodded soberly. 'I had to. It was all I could do. I wrote stories about my own real world. To those other people my tales were wild imaginations – and they liked them.'

We chuckled. But Carrick was deadly serious.

Madison humoured him to the end. 'And how did you finally get back home from that other world you'd created?'

'I never did get back home,' Carrick said with a heavy sigh.

'Oh, come now,' Madison protested lightly. 'It's obvious that you got back some time.'

Carrick shook his head somberly as he rose to leave.

'No, I never got back home,' he said soberly. 'I'm still here.'

The Star

ARTHUR C. CLARKE

It is three thousand light-years to the Vatican. Once, I believed that space could have no power over faith, just as I believed that the heavens declared the glory of God's handiwork. Now I have seen that handiwork, and my faith is sorely troubled. I stare at the crucifix that hangs on the cabin wall above the Mark VI Computer, and for the first time in my life I wonder if it is no more than an empty symbol.

I have told no one yet, but the truth cannot be concealed. The facts are there for all to read, recorded on the countless miles of magnetic tape and the thousands of photographs we are carrying back to Earth. Other scientists can interpret them as easily as I can, and I am not one who would condone that tampering with the truth which often gave my order a bad name in the olden days.

The crew are already sufficiently depressed: I wonder how they will take this ultimate irony. Few of them have any religious faith, yet they will not relish using this final weapon in their campaign against me – that private, good-natured, but fundamentally serious, war which lasted all the way from Earth. It amused them to have a Jesuit as chief astrophysicist: Dr Chandler, for instance, could never get over it. (Why are medical men such notorious atheists?) Sometimes he would meet me on the observation deck, where the lights are always low so that the stars shine with undiminished glory. He would come up to me in the gloom and stand staring out of the great oval port, while the heavens crawled slowly around us as the ship turned end over end with the residual spin we had never bothered to correct.

'Well, Father,' he would say at last, 'it goes on forever and forever, and perhaps *Something* made it. But how you can believe that Something has a special interest in us and our miserable little world – that just beats me.' Then the argument would start, while the stars and nebulae would swing around us in silent, endless arcs beyond the flawlessly clear plastic of the observation port.

It was, I think, the apparent incongruity of my position that caused most amusement to the crew. In vain I would point to my three papers in the *Astrophysical Journal*, my five in the *Monthly Notices of the Royal Astronomical Society*. I would remind them that my order has long been famous for its scientific works. We may be few now, but ever since the eighteenth century we have made contributions to astronomy and geophysics out of all proportion to our numbers. Will my report on the Phoenix Nebula end our thousand years of history? It will end, I fear, much more than that.

I do not know who gave the nebula its name, which seems to me a very bad one. If it contains a prophecy, it is one that cannot be verified for several billion years. Even the word nebula is misleading: this is a far smaller object than those stupendous clouds of mist – the stuff of unborn stars – that are scattered throughout the length of the Milky Way. On the cosmic scale, indeed, the Phoenix Nebula is a tiny thing – a tenuous shell of gas surrounding a single star.

Or what is left of a star . . .

The Rubens engraving of Loyola seems to mock me as it hangs there above the spectrophotometer tracings. What would *you*, Father, have made of this knowledge that has come into my keeping, so far from the little world that was all the universe you knew? Would your faith have risen to the challenge, as mine has failed to do?

You gaze into the distance, Father, but I have travelled a distance beyond any that you could have imagined when you founded our order a thousand years ago. No other survey ship has been so far from Earth: we are at the very frontiers of the explored universe. We set out to reach the Phoenix Nebula, we succeeded, and we are homeward bound with our burden of knowledge. I wish I could lift that burden from my shoulders, but I call to you in vain across the centuries and the light-years that lie between us.

On the book you are holding the words are plain to read. AD MAIOREM DEI GLORIAM, the message runs, but it is a message I can no longer believe. Would you still believe it, if you could see what we have found?

We knew, of course, what the Phoenix Nebula was. Every year, in our galaxy alone, more than a hundred stars explode, blazing for a few hours or days with thousands of times their normal brilliance before they sink back into death and obscurity. Such are the ordinary novae – the commonplace disasters of the universe. I have recorded the spectrograms and light curves of dozens since I started working at the Lunar Observatory.

But three or four times in every thousand years occurs something beside which even a nova pales into total insignificance.

When a star becomes a *supernova*, it may for a little while outshine all the massed suns of the galaxy. The Chinese astronomers watched this happen in AD 1054, not knowing what it was they saw. Five centuries later, in 1572, a supernova blazed in Cassiopeia so brilliantly that it was visible in the daylight sky. There have been three more in the thousand years that have passed since then.

Our mission was to visit the remnants of such a catastrophe, to reconstruct the events that led up to it, and, if possible, to learn its cause. We came slowly in through the concentric shells of gas that had been blasted out six thousand years before, yet were expanding still. They were immensely hot, radiating even now with a fierce violet light, but were far too tenuous to do us any damage. When the star had exploded, its outer layers had been driven upwards with such speed that they had escaped completely from its gravitational field. Now they formed a hollow shell large enough to engulf a thousand solar systems, and at its centre burned the tiny, fantastic object which the star had now become – a white dwarf, smaller than the Earth, yet weighing a million times as much.

The glowing gas shells were all around us, banishing the normal night of interstellar space. We were flying into the centre of a cosmic bomb that had detonated millennia ago and whose incandescent fragments were still hurtling apart. The immense scale of the explosion, and the fact that the debris already covered a volume of space many billions of miles across, robbed the scene of any visible movement. It would take decades before the unaided eye could detect any motion in these tortured wisps and eddies of gas, yet the sense of turbulent expansion was overwhelming.

We had checked our primary drive hours before, and were drifting slowly towards the fierce little star ahead. Once it had been a sun like our own, but it had squandered in a few hours the energy that should have kept it shining for a million years. Now it was a shrunken miser, hoarding its resources as if trying to make amends for its prodigal youth.

No one seriously expected to find planets. If there had been any before the explosion, they would have been boiled into puffs of vapour, and their substance lost in the greater wreckage of the star itself. But we made the automatic search, as we always do when approaching an unknown sun, and presently we found a single small world circling the star at an immense distance. It must have been the Pluto of this vanished solar system, orbiting on the frontiers of the night. Too far from the central sun ever to have known life, its remoteness had saved it from the fate of all its lost companions.

The passing fires had seared its rocks and burned away the mantle of frozen gas that must have covered it in the days before the disaster. We landed, and we found the Vault.

Its builders had made sure that we should. The monolithic marker that stood above the entrance was now a fused stump, but even the first long-range photographs told us that here was the work of intelligence. A little later we detected the continent-wide pattern of radioactivity that had been buried in the rock. Even if the pylon above the Vault had been destroyed, this would have remained, an immovable and all but eternal beacon calling to the stars. Our ship fell towards this gigantic bull's-eye like an arrow into its target.

The pylon must have been a mile high when it was built, but now it looked like a candle that had melted down into a puddle of wax. It took us a week to drill through the fused rock, since we did not have the proper tools for a task like this. We were astronomers, not archaeologists, but we could improvise. Our original purpose was forgotten: this lonely monument, reared with such labour at the greatest possible distance from the doomed sun, could have only one meaning. A civilization that knew it was about to die had made its last bid for immortality.

It will take us generations to examine all the treasures that were placed in the Vault. They had plenty of time to prepare, for their sun must have given its first warning many years before the final detonation. Everything that they wished to preserve, all the fruit of their genius, they brought here to this distant world in the days before the end, hoping that some other race would find it and that they would not be utterly forgotten. Would we have done as well, or would we have been too lost in our own misery to give thought to a future we could never see or share?

If only they had had a little more time! They could travel freely enough between the planets of their own sun, but they had not yet learned to cross the interstellar gulfs, and the nearest solar system was a hundred light-years away. Yet even had they possessed a secret of the Transfinite Drive no more than a few millions could have been saved. Perhaps it was better thus.

Even if they had not been so disturbingly human as their sculpture shows, we could not have helped admiring them and grieving for their fate. They left thousands of visual records and the machines for projecting them, together with elaborate pictorial instructions from which it will not be difficult to learn their written language. We have examined many of these records, and brought to life for the first time in six thousand years the warmth and beauty of a civilization that in many ways must have been superior to our own. Perhaps they only showed us the best, and one can hardly blame them. But their worlds were very lovely, and their cities were built with a grace that matches anything of man's. We have watched them at work and play, and listened to their musical speech sounding across the centuries.

One scene is still before my eyes – a group of children on a beach of strange blue sand, playing in the waves as children play on Earth. Curious whiplike trees line the shore, and some very large animal is wading in the shallows yet attracting no attention at all.

And sinking into the sea, still warm and friendly and life-giving, is the sun that will turn traitor and obliterate all this innocent happiness.

Perhaps if we had not been so far from home and so vulnerable to loneliness, we should not have been so deeply moved. Many of us had seen the ruins of ancient civilizations on other worlds, but they had never affected us so profoundly. This tragedy was unique. It is one thing for a race to fail and die, as nations and cultures have done on Earth. But to be destroyed so completely in the full flower of its achievement, leaving no survivors – now could that be reconciled with the mercy of God?

My colleagues have asked me that, and I have given what answers I can. Perhaps you could have done better, Father Loyola, but I have found nothing in the *Exercitia Spiritualia* that helps me here. They were not an evil people: I do not know what gods they worshipped, if indeed they worshipped any. But I have looked back at them across the centuries, and have watched while the loveliness they used their last strength to preserve was brought forth again into the light of their shrunken sun. They could have taught us much: why were they destroyed?

I know the answers that my colleagues will give when they get back to Earth. They will say that the universe has no purpose and no plan, that since a hundred suns explode every year in our galaxy, at this very moment some race is dying in the depths of space. Whether that race has done good or evil during its lifetime will make no difference in the end: there is no divine justice, for there is no God.

Yet, of course, what we have seen proves nothing of the sort. Anyone who argues thus is being swayed by emotion, not logic. God has no need to justify His actions to man. He who built the universe can destroy it when He chooses. It is arrogance – it is perilously near blasphemy – for us to say what He may or may not do.

This I could have accepted, hard though it is to look upon whole worlds and peoples thrown into the furnace. But there comes a point when even the deepest faith must falter, and now, as I look at the calculations lying before me, I know I have reached that point at last.

We could not tell, before we reached the nebula, how long ago the explosion took place. Now, from the astronomical evidence and the record in the rocks of that one surviving planet, I have been able to date it very exactly. I know in what year the light of this colossal conflagration reached our Earth. I know how brilliantly the supernova whose corpse now dwindles behind our speeding ship once shone in terrestrial skies. I know how it must have blazed low in the east before sunrise, like a beacon in that oriental dawn.

There can be no reasonable doubt: the ancient mystery is solved at last. Yet, oh God, there were so many stars you could have used. What was the need to give these people to the fire, that the symbol of their passing might shine above Bethlehem?

All Summer in a Day

RAY BRADBURY

'Ready?'

'Ready.'

'Now?'

'Soon!'

'Do the scientists really know? Will it happen today, will it?'

'Look, look; see for yourself!'

The children pressed to each other like so many roses, so many weeds, intermixed, peering out for a look at the hidden sun.

It rained.

It had been raining for seven years; thousands upon thousands of days compounded and filled from one end to the other with rain, with the drum and gush of water, with the sweet crystal fall of showers and the concussion of storms so heavy they were tidal waves come over the islands. A thousand forests had been crushed under the rain and grown up a thousand times to be crushed again. And this was the way life was forever on the planet Venus, and this was the schoolroom of the children of the rocket men and women who had come to a raining world to set up civilization and live out their lives.

'It's stopping, it's stopping!'

'Yes, yes!'

Margot stood apart from them, from these children who could never remember a time when there wasn't rain and rain and rain. They were all nine years old, and if there had been a day, seven years ago, when the sun came out for an hour and showed its face to the stunned world, they could not recall. Sometimes, at night, she heard them stir, in remembrance, and she knew they were dreaming and remembering gold or a yellow crayon or a coin large enough to buy the world with. She knew that they thought they remembered a warmness, like a blushing in the face, in the body, in the arms and legs and trembling hands. But then they always awoke to the tatting drum, the endless shaking down of clear bead necklaces upon the roof, the walk, the gardens, the forest, and their dreams were gone.

All day yesterday they had read in class, about the sun. About how like a lemon it was, and how hot. And they had written small stories or essays or poems about it:

> 'I think the sun is a flower,
> That blooms for just one hour.'

That was Margot's poem, read in a quiet voice in the still classroom while the rain was falling outside.

'Aw, you didn't write that!' protested one of the boys.

'I did,' said Margot. 'I *did*.'

'William!' said the teacher.

But that was yesterday. Now, the rain was slackening, and the children were crushed to the great thick windows.

'Where's teacher?'

'She'll be back.'

'She'd better hurry, we'll miss it!'

They turned on themselves, like a feverish wheel, all tumbling spokes.

Margot stood alone. She was a very frail girl who looked as if she had been lost in the rain for years and the rain had washed out the blue from her eyes and the red from her mouth and the yellow from her hair.

She was an old photograph dusted from an album, whitened away, and if she spoke at all her voice would be a ghost. Now she stood, separate, staring at the rain and the loud wet world beyond the huge glass.

'What're *you* looking at?' said William.

Margot said nothing.

'Speak when you're spoken to.' He gave her a shove. But she did not move; rather, she let herself be moved only by him and nothing else.

They edged away from her, they would not look at her. She felt them go away. And this was because she would play no games with them in the echoing tunnels of the underground city. If they tagged her and ran, she stood blinking after them and did not follow. When the class sang songs about happiness and life and games, her lips barely moved. Only when they sang about the sun and the summer did her lips move, as she watched the drenched windows.

And then, of course, the biggest crime of all was that she had come here only five years ago from Earth, and she remembered the sun and the way the sun was and the sky was, when she was four, in Ohio. And they, they had been on Venus all their lives, and they had been only two years old when the last sun came out, and had long since forgotten the colour and heat of it and the way that it really was. But Margot remembered.

'It's like a penny,' she said, once, eyes closed.

'No it's not!' the children cried.

'It's like a fire,' she said, 'in the stove.'

'You're lying, you don't remember!' cried the children.

But she remembered and stood quietly apart from all of them, and watched the patterning windows. And once, a month ago, she had refused to shower in the school shower rooms, had clutched her hands to her ears and over her head, screaming the water mustn't touch her head. So after that, dimly, dimly, she sensed it, she was different and they knew her difference and kept away.

There was talk that her father and mother were taking her back to Earth next year; it seemed vital to her that they do so, though it would mean the loss of thousands of dollars to her family. And so, the children hated her for all these reasons, of big and little consequence. They hated her pale snow face, her waiting silence, her thinness and her possible future.

'Get away!' The boy gave her another push. 'What're you waiting for?'

Then, for the first time, she turned and looked at him. And what she was waiting for was in her eyes.

'Well, don't wait around here!' cried the boy, savagely. 'You won't see nothing!'

Her lips moved.

'Nothing!' he cried. 'It was all a joke, wasn't it?' He turned to the other children. 'Nothing's happening today. *Is* it?'

They all blinked at him and then, understanding, laughed and shook their heads. 'Nothing, nothing!'

'Oh, but,' Margot whispered, her eyes helpless. 'But, this is the day, the scientists predict, they say, they *know*, the sun . . .'

'All a joke!' said the boy, and seized her roughly. 'Hey, everyone, let's put her in a closet before teacher comes!'

'No,' said Margot, falling back.

They surged about her, caught her up and bore her, protesting, and then pleading, and then crying, back into a tunnel, a room, a closet, where they slammed and locked the door. They stood looking at the door and saw it tremble from her beating and throwing herself against it. They heard her muffled cries. Then, smiling, they turned and went out and back down the tunnel, just as the teacher arrived.

'Ready, children?' She glanced at her watch.

'Yes!' said everyone.

'Are we all here?'

'Yes!'

The rain slackened still more.

They crowded to the huge door.

The rain stopped.

It was as if, in the midst of a film concerning an avalanche, a tornado, a hurricane, a volcanic eruption, something had, first, gone wrong with the sound apparatus, thus muffling and finally cutting off all noise, all of the blasts and repercussions and thunders, and then, secondly, ripped the film from the projector and inserted in its place a peaceful tropical slide which did not move or tremor. The world ground to a standstill. The silence was so immense and unbelievable that you felt your ears had been stuffed or you had lost your hearing altogether. The children put their hands to their ears. They stood apart. The door slid back and the smell of the silent, waiting world came in to them.

The sun came out.

It was the colour of flaming bronze and it was very large. And the sky around it was a blazing blue tile colour. And the jungle burned with sunlight as the children, released from their spell, rushed out, yelling, into the summertime.

'Now, don't go too far,' called the teacher after them. 'You've only one hour, you know. You wouldn't want to get caught out!'

But they were running and turning their faces up to the sky and feeling the sun on their cheeks like a warm iron; they were taking off their jackets and letting the sun burn their arms.

'Oh, it's better than the sunlamps, isn't it?'

'Much, much better!'

They stopped running and stood in the great

jungle that covered Venus, that grew and never stopped growing, tumultuously, even as you watched it. It was a nest of octupuses, clustering up great arms of flesh-like weed, wavering, flowering in this brief spring. It was the colour of rubber and ash, this jungle from the many years without sun. It was the colour of stones and white cheeses and ink.

The children lay out, laughing, on the jungle mattress, and heard it sigh and squeak under them, resilient and alive. They ran among the trees, they slipped and fell, they pushed each other, they played hide-and-seek and tag but most of all they squinted at the sun until tears ran down their faces, they put their hands up at that yellowness and that amazing blueness and they breathed of the fresh fresh air and listened and listened to the silence which suspended them in a blessed sea of no sound and no motion. They looked at everything and savoured everything. Then, wildly, like animals escaped from their caves, they ran and ran in shouting circles. They ran for an hour and did not stop running.

And then –

In the midst of their running, one of the girls wailed.

Everyone stopped.

The girl, standing in the open, held out her hand.

'Oh, look, look,' she said, trembling.

They came slowly to look at her opened palm.

In the centre of it, cupped and huge, was a single raindrop.

She began to cry, looking at it.

They glanced quickly at the sky.

'Oh. Oh.'

A few cold drops fell on their noses and their cheeks and their mouths. The sun faded behind a stir of mist. A wind blew cool around them. They turned and started to walk back toward their underground house, their hands at their sides, their smiles vanishing away.

A boom of thunder startled them and like leaves before a new hurricane, they tumbled upon each other and ran. Lightning struck ten miles away, five miles away, a mile, a half-mile. The sky darkened into midnight in a flash.

They stood in the doorway of the underground house for a moment until it was raining hard. Then they closed the door and heard the gigantic sound of the rain falling in tons and avalanches everywhere and forever.

'Will it be seven more years?'

'Yes, seven.'

Then one of them gave a little cry.

'Margot!'

'What?'

'She's still in the closet where we locked her.'

'Margot.'

They stood as if someone had driven them, like so many stakes, into the floor. They looked at each other and then looked away. They glanced out at the world that was raining now and raining and raining steadily. They could not meet each other's glances. Their faces were solemn and pale. They looked at their hands and feet, their faces down.

'Margot.'

One of the girls said, 'Well . . .?'

No one moved.

'Go on,' whispered the girl.

They walked slowly down the hall in the sound of cold rain. They turned through the doorway to the room, in the sound of the storm and thunder, lightning on their faces, blue and terrible. They walked over to the closet door slowly and stood by it.

Behind the closet door was only silence.

They unlocked the door, even more slowly, and let Margot out.

Protected Species

H. B. FYFE

The yellow star, of which Torang was the second planet, shone hotly down on the group of men viewing the half-built dam from the heights above. At a range of eighty million miles, the effect was quite Terran, the star being somewhat smaller than Sol.

For Jeff Otis, fresh from a hop through space from the extra-bright star that was the other component of the binary system, the heat was enervating. The shorts and light shirt supplied him by the planet coordinator were soaked with perspiration. He mopped his forehead and turned to his host.

'Very nice job, Finchley,' he complimented. 'It's easy to see you have things well in hand here.'

Finchley grinned sparingly. He had a broad, hard, flat face with tight lips and mere slits of blue eyes. Otis had been trying ever since the previous morning to catch a revealing expression on it.

He was uneasily aware that his own features were too frank and open for an inspector of colonial installations. For one thing, he had too many lines and hollows in his face, a result of being chronically underweight from space-hopping among the sixteen planets of the binary system.

Otis noticed that Finchley's aides were eyeing him furtively.

'Yes, Finchley,' he repeated to break the little silence, 'you're doing very well on the hydroelectric end. When are you going to show me the capital city you're laying out?'

'We can fly over there now,' answered Finchley. 'We have tentative boundaries laid out below those precolony ruins we saw from the 'copter.'

'Oh, yes. You know, I meant to remark as we flew over that they looked a good deal like similar remnants on some of the other planets.'

He caught himself as Finchley's thin lips tightened a trifle more. The coordinator was obviously trying to be patient and polite to an official from whom he hoped to get a good report, but Otis could see he would much rather be going about his business of building up the colony.

He could hardly blame Finchley, he decided. It was the fifth planetary system Terrans had found in their expansion into space, and there would be bigger jobs ahead for a man with a record of successful accomplishments. Civilization was reaching out to the stars at last. Otis supposed that he, too, was some sort of pioneer, although he usually was too busy to feel like one.

'Well, I'll show you some photos later,' he said. 'Right now, we – Say, why all that jet-burning down there?'

In the gorge below, men had dropped their tools and seemed to be charging toward a common focal point. Excited yells carried thinly up the cliffs.

'Ape hunt, probably,' guessed one of Finchley's engineers.

'Ape?' asked Otis, surprised.

'Not exactly,' corrected Finchley patiently. 'That's common slang for what we mention in reports as Torangs. They look a little like big, skinny, grey apes; but they're the only life large enough to name after the planet.'

Otis stared down into the gorge. Most of the running men had given up and were straggling back to their work. Two or three, brandishing pistols, continued running and disappeared around a bend.

'Never catch him now,' commented Finchley's pilot.

'Do you just let them go running off whenever they feel like it?' Otis inquired.

Finchley met his curious gaze stolidly.

'I'm in favour of anything that will break the monotony, Mr Otis. We have a problem of morale, you know. This planet is a key colony, and I like to keep the work going smoothly.'

'Yes, I suppose there isn't much for recreation yet.'

'Exactly. I don't see the sport in it myself but I let them. We're up to schedule.'

'Ahead, if anything,' Otis placated him. 'Well, now, about the city?'

Finchley led the way to the helicopter. The pilot and Otis waited while he had a final word with his engineers, then they all climbed in and were off.

Later, hovering over the network of crude roads being levelled by Finchley's bulldozers, Otis admitted aloud that the location was well chosen. It lay along a long, narrow bay that thrust in from the distant ocean to gather the waters of the same river that was being dammed some miles upstream.

'Those cliffs over there,' Finchley pointed out, 'were raised up since the end of whatever civilization used to be here – so my geologist tells me. We can fly back that way, and you can see how the ancient city was once at the head of the bay.'

The pilot climbed and headed over the cliffs. Otis saw that these formed the edge of a plateau. At one point, their continuity was marred by a deep gorge.

'Where the river ran thousands of years ago,' Finchley explained.

They reached a point from which the outlines of the ruined city were easily discerned. From the air, Otis knew, they were undoubtedly plainer than if he had been among them.

'Must have been a pretty large place,' he remarked. 'Any idea what sort of beings built it or what happened to them?'

'Haven't had time for that yet,' Finchley said. 'Some boys from the exploration staff poke around in there every so often. Best current theory seems to be that it belonged to the Torangs.'

'The *animals* they were hunting before?' asked Otis.

'Might be. Can't say for sure, but the diggers found signs the city took more of a punch than just an earthquake. Claim they found too much evidence of fires, exploded missiles, and warfare in general – other places as well as here. So . . . we've been guessing the Torangs are degenerated descendants of the survivors of some interplanetary brawl.'

Otis considered that.

'Sounds plausible,' he admitted, 'but you ought to do something to make sure you are right.'

'Why?'

'If it *is* the case, you'll have to stop your men from hunting them; degenerated or not, the Colonial Commission has regulations about contact with any local inhabitants.'

Finchley turned his head to scowl at Otis, and controlled himself with an obvious effort.

'Those *apes*?' he demanded.

'Well, how can you tell? Ever try to contact them?'

'Yes! At first, that is; before we figured them for animals.'

'And?'

'Couldn't get near one!' Finchley declared heatedly. 'If they had any sort of half-intelligent culture, wouldn't they let us make *some* sort of contact?'

'Offhand,' admitted Otis, 'I should think so. How about setting down a few minutes? I'd like to look at the ruins.'

Finchley glared at his wrist watch, but directed the pilot to land at a cleared spot. The young man brought them down neatly and the two officials alighted.

Otis, glancing around, saw where the archaeologists had been digging. They had left their implements stacked casually at the site – the air was dry up here and who was there to steal a shovel?

He left Finchley and strolled around a mound of dirt that had been cleared away from an entrance to one of the buildings. The latter had been built of stone, or at least faced with it. A peep into the dim excavation led him to believe there had been a steel framework, but the whole affair had been collapsed as if by an explosion.

He walked a little way further and reached a section of presumably taller buildings where the stone ruins thrust above the sandy surface. After he had wandered through one or two arched openings that seemed to have been windows, he understood why the explorers had chosen to dig for their information. If any covering or decoration had ever graced the walls, it had long since been weathered off. As for ceiling or roof, nothing remained.

'Must have been a highly developed civilization just the same,' he muttered.

A movement at one of the shadowed openings to his right caught his eye. He did not remember noticing Finchley leave the helicopter to follow him, but he was glad of a guide.

'Don't you think so?' he added.

He turned his head, but Finchley was not there. In fact, now that Otis was aware of his surroundings, he could hear the voices of the other two mumbling distantly back by the aircraft.

'Seeing things!' he grumbled, and started through the ancient window.

Some instinct stopped him half a foot outside.

Come on, Jeff, he told himself, *don't be silly! What could be there? Ghosts?*

On the other hand, he realized, there were times when it was just as well to rely upon instinct – at least until you figured out the origin of the strange feeling. Any spaceman would agree to that. The man who developed an animal sixth sense was the man who lived longest on alien planets.

He thought he must have paused a full minute or more, during which he had heard not the slightest sound except the mutter of voices to the rear. He peered into the chamber, which was about twenty feet square and well if not brightly lit by reflected light.

Nothing was to be seen, but when he found himself turning his head stealthily to peer over his shoulder, he decided that the queer sensation along the back of his neck meant something.

Wait, now, he thought swiftly. *I didn't see quite the whole room.*

The flooring was heaped with wind-bared rubble that would not show footprints. He felt much more comfortable to notice himself thinking in that vein.

At least, I'm not imagining ghosts, he thought.

Bending forward the necessary foot, he thrust his head through the opening and darted a quick look to left, then to the right along the wall. As he turned right, his glance was met directly by a pair of very wide-set black eyes which shifted inward slightly as they got his range.

The Torang about matched his own six-feet-two, mainly because of elongated, gibbonlike limbs and a similarly crouching stance. Arms and legs, covered with short, curly, grey fur, had the same general proportions as human limbs, but looked half again too long for a trunk that seemed to be ribbed all the way down. Shoulder and hip joints were compactly lean, rather as if the Torang had developed on a world of lesser gravity than that of the human.

It was the face that made Otis stare. The mouth was toothless and probably constructed more for sucking than for chewing. But the eyes! They projected like ends of a dumb-bell from each side of the narrow skull where the ears should have been, and focused with obvious mobility. Peering closer, Otis saw tiny ears below the eyes, almost hidden in the curling fur of the neck.

He realized abruptly that his own eyes felt as if they were bulging out, although he could not remember having changed his expression of casual curiosity. His back was getting stiff also. He straightened up carefully.

'Uh . . . hello,' he murmured, feeling unutterably silly but conscious of some impulse to compromise between a tone of greeting for another human being and one of pacification to an animal.

The Torang moved then, swiftly but unhurriedly. In fact, Otis later decided, deliberately. One of the long arms swept downward to the rubble-strewn ground.

The next instant, Otis jerked his head back out of the opening as a stone whizzed past in front of his nose.

'Hey!' he protested involuntarily.

There was a scrabbling sound from within, as of animal claws churning to a fast start among the pebbles. Recovering his balance, Otis charged recklessly through the entrance.

'I don't know why,' he admitted to Finchley a few minutes later. 'If I stopped to think how I might have had my skull bashed in coming through, I guess I'd have just backed off and yelled for you.'

Finchley nodded, but his narrow gaze seemed faintly approving for the first time since they had met.

'He was gone, of course,' Otis continued. 'I barely caught a glimpse of his rump vanishing through another window.'

'Yeah, they're pretty fast,' put in Finchley's pilot. 'In the time we've been here, the boys haven't taken more than half a dozen. Got a stuffed one over at headquarters though.'

'Hm-m-m,' murmured Otis thoughtfully.

From their other remarks, he learned that he had not noticed everything, even though face to face with the creature. Finchley's mentioning the three digits of the hands or feet, for instance, came as a surprise.

Otis was silent most of the flight back to headquarters. Once there, he disappeared with a perfunctory excuse towards the rooms assigned him.

That evening, at a dinner which Finchley had made as attractive as was possible in a comparatively raw and new colony, Otis was noticeably sociable. The coordinator was gratified.

'Looks as if they finally sent us a regular guy,' he remarked behind his hand to one of his assistants. 'Round up a couple of the prettier secretaries to keep him happy.'

'I understand he nearly laid hands on a Torang up at the diggings,' said the other.

'Yep, ran right at it bare-handed. Came as close

to bagging it as anybody could, I suppose.'

'Maybe it's just as well he didn't,' commented the assistant. 'They're big enough to mess up an unarmed man some.'

Otis, meanwhile and for the rest of the evening, was assiduously busy making acquaintances. So engrossed was he in turning every new conversation to the Torangs and asking seemingly casual questions about the little known of their habits and possible past, that he hardly noticed receiving any special attentions. As a visiting inspector, he was used to attempts to entertain and distract him.

The next morning, he caught Finchley at his office in the sprawling one-storey structure of concrete and glass that was colonial headquarters.

After accepting a chair across the desk from the coordinator, Otis told him his conclusions. Finchley's narrow eyes opened a trifle when he heard the details. His wide, hard-muscled face became slightly pink.

'Oh, for –! I mean, Otis, why must you make something big out of it? The men very seldom bag one anyway!'

'Perhaps because they're so rare,' answered Otis calmly. 'How do we know they're not intelligent life? Maybe if you were hanging on in the ruins of your ancestors' civilization, reduced to a primitive state, *you'd* be just as wary of a bunch of loud Terrans moving in!'

Finchley shrugged. He looked vaguely uncomfortable, as if debating whether Otis or some disgruntled sportsman from his husky construction crews would be easier to handle.

'Think of the overall picture a minute,' Otis urged. 'We're pushing out into space at last, after centuries of dreams and struggles. With all the misery we've seen in various colonial systems at home, we've tried to plan these ventures so as to avoid old mistakes.'

Finchley nodded grudgingly. Otis could see that his mind was on the progress charts of his many projects.

'It stands to reason,' the inspector went on, 'that some day we'll find a planet with intelligent life. We're still new in space, but as we probe farther out, it's bound to happen. That's why the Commission drew up rules about native life forms. Or haven't you read that part of the code lately?'

Finchley shifted from side to side in his chair.

'Now, look!' he protested. 'Don't go making *me* out a hardboiled vandal with nothing in mind but exterminating everything that moves on all Torang. *I* don't go out hunting the apes!'

'I know, I know,' Otis soothed him. 'But before the Colonial Commission will sanction any destruction of indigenous life, we'll have to show – *besides* that it's not intelligent – that it exists in sufficient numbers to avoid extinction.'

'What do you expect me to do about it?'

Otis regarded him with some sympathy. Finchley was the hard-bitten type the Commission needed to oversee the first breaking-in of a colony on a strange planet, but he was not unreasonable. He merely wanted to be left alone to handle the tough job facing him.

'Announce a ban on hunting Torangs,' Otis said. 'There must be something else they can go after.'

'Oh, yes,' admitted Finchley. 'There are swarms of little rabbit-things and other vermin running through the brush. But, I don't know –'

'It's standard practice,' Otis reminded him. 'We have many a protected species even back on Terra that would be extinct by now, but for the game laws.'

In the end, they agreed that Finchley would do his honest best to enforce a ban provided Otis obtained a formal order from the headquarters of the system. The inspector went from the office straight to the communications centre, where he filed a long report for the chief coordinator's office in the other part of the binary system.

It took some hours for the reply to reach Torang. When it came that afternoon, he went looking for Finchley.

He found the coordinator inspecting a newly finished canning factory on the coast, elated at the completion of one more link in making the colony self-sustaining.

'Here it is,' said Otis, waving the message copy. 'Signed by the chief himself. "As of this date, the apelike beings known as Torangs, indigenous to planet number and so forth, are to be considered a rare and protected species under regulations and so forth et cetera."'

'Good enough,' answered Finchley with an amiable shrug. 'Give it here, and I'll have it put on the public address system and the bulletin boards.'

Otis returned satisfied to the helicopter that had brought him out from headquarters.

'Back, sir?' asked the pilot.

'Yes . . . *no*! Just for fun, take me out to the old city. I never did get a good look the other day, and I'd like to before I leave.'

They flew over the plains between the sea and the upjutting cliffs. In the distance, Otis caught a glimpse of the rising dam he had been shown the day before. This colony would go well, he reflected, as long as he checked up on details like preserving native life forms.

Eventually, the pilot landed at the same spot he had been taken on his previous visit to the ancient ruins.

Someone else was on the scene today. Otis saw a pair of men he took to be archaeologists.

'I'll just wander around a bit,' he told the pilot.

He noticed the two men looking at him from where they stood by the shovels and other equipment, so he paused to say hello. As he thought, they had been digging in the ruins.

'Taking some measurements in fact,' said the sunburned blond introduced as Hoffman. 'Trying to get a line on what sort of things built the place.'

'Oh?' said Otis, interested. 'What's the latest theory?'

'Not so much different from us,' Hoffman told the inspector while his partner left them to pick up another load of artefacts.

'Judging from the size of the rooms, height of doorways, and such stuff as stairways,' he went on, 'they were pretty much our size. So far, of course, it's only a rough estimate.'

'Could be ancestors of the Torangs, eh?' asked Otis.

'Very possible, sir,' answered Hoffman, with a promptness that suggested it was his own view. 'But we haven't dug up enough to guess at the type of culture they had, or draw any conclusions as to their psychology or social customs.'

Otis nodded, thinking that he ought to mention the young fellow's name to Finchley before he left Torang. He excused himself as the other man returned with a box of some sort of scraps the pair had unearthed, and strolled between the outlines of the untouched buildings.

In a few minutes, he came to the section of higher structures where he had encountered the Torang the previous day.

'Wonder if I should look in the same spot?' he

muttered aloud. 'No . . . that would be the *last* place the thing would return to . . . unless it had a lair thereabouts –'

He stopped to get his bearings, then shrugged and walked around a mound of rubble toward what he believed to be the proper building.

Pretty sure this was it, he mused. *Yes, shadows around that window arch look the same . . . same time of day –*

He halted, almost guiltily, and looked back to make sure no one was observing his return to the scene of his little adventure. After all, an inspector of colonial installations was not supposed to run around ghost-hunting like a small boy.

Finding himself alone, he stepped briskly through the crumbling arch – *and froze in his tracks.*

'I am honoured to know you,' said the Torang in a mild, rather buzzing voice. 'We thought you possibly would return here.'

Otis gaped. The black eyes projecting from the sides of the narrow head tracked him up and down, giving him the unpleasant sensation of being measured for an artillery salvo.

'I am known as Jal-Ganyr,' said the Torang. 'Unless I am given incorrect data, you are known as Jeff-Otis. That is so.'

The last statement was made with almost no inflection, but some still-functioning corner of Otis's mind interpreted it as a question. He sucked in a deep breath, suddenly conscious of having forgotten to breathe for a moment.

'I didn't know . . . yes, that is so . . . I didn't know you Torangs could speak Terran. Or anything else. How –?'

He hesitated as a million questions boiled up in his mind to be asked. Jal-Ganyr absently stroked the grey fur of his chest with his three-fingered left hand, squatting patiently on a flat rock. Otis felt somehow that he had been allowed to waste time mumbling only by grace of disciplined politeness.

'I am not of the Torangs,' said Jal-Ganyr in his wheezing voice. 'I am of the Myrbs. You would possibly say Myrbii. I have not been informed.'

'You mean that is your name for yourselves?' asked Otis.

Jal-Ganyr seemed to consider, his mobile eyes swivelling inward to scan the Terran's face.

'More than that,' he said at last, when he had thought it over. 'I mean I am of the race originating at Myrb, not of this planet.'

'Before we go any further,' insisted Otis, 'tell me, at least, how you learned our language!'

Jal-Ganyr made a fleeting gesture. His 'face' was unreadable to the Terran, but Otis had the impression he had received the equivalent of a smile and a shrug.

'As to that,' said the Myrb, 'I possibly learned it before you did. We have observed you a very long time. You would unbelieve how long.'

'But then –' Otis paused. That must mean before the colonists had landed on this planet. He was half-afraid it might mean before they had reached this sun system. He put aside the thought and asked, 'But then, why do you live like this among the ruins? Why wait till now? If you had communicated, you could have had our help rebuilding –'

He let his voice trail off, wondering what sounded wrong. Jal-Ganyr rolled his eyes about leisurely, as if disdaining the surrounding ruins. Again, he seemed to consider all the implications of Otis's questions.

'We picked up your message to your chief,' he answered at last. 'We decided time is to communicate with one of you.'

'We have no interest in rebuilding,' he added. 'We have concealed quarters for ourselves.'

Otis found that his lips were dry from his unconsciously having let his mouth hang open. He moistened them with the tip of his tongue, and relaxed enough to lean against the wall.

'You mean my getting the ruling to proclaim you a protected species?' he asked. 'You have instruments to intercept such signals?'

'I do. We have,' said Jal-Ganyr simply. 'It has been decided that you have expanded far enough into space to make necessary we contact a few of the thoughtful among you. It will possibly make easier in the future for our observers.'

Otis wondered how much of that was irony. He felt himself flushing at the memory of the 'stuffed specimen' at headquarters, and was pecularily relieved that he had not gone to see it.

I've had the luck, he told himself. *I'm the one to discover the first known intelligent beings beyond Sol!*

Aloud, he said, 'We expected to meet someone like you eventually. But why have you chosen me?'

The question sounded vain, he realized, but it brought unexpected results.

'Your message. You made in a little way the same decision we made in a big way. We deduce that you are one to understand our regret and shame at what happened between our races . . . long ago.'

'Between –'

'Yes. For a long time, we thought you were all gone. We are pleased to see you returning to some of your old planets.'

Otis stared blankly. Some instinct must have enabled the Myrb to interpret his bewildered expression. He apologized briefly.

'I possibly forgot to explain the ruins.' Again, Jal-Ganyr's eyes swivelled slowly about.

'They are not ours,' he said mildly. 'They are yours.'

History Lesson

ARTHUR C. CLARKE

No one could remember when the tribe had begun its long journey. The land of great rolling plains that had been its first home was now no more than a half-forgotten dream.

For many years Shann and his people had been fleeing through a country of low hills and sparkling lakes, and now the mountains lay ahead. This summer they must cross them to the southern lands. There was little time to lose. The white terror that had come down from the Poles, grinding continents to dust and freezing the very air before it, was less than a day's march behind.

Shann wondered if the glaciers could climb the mountains ahead, and within his heart he dared to kindle a little flame of hope. This might prove a barrier against which even the remorseless ice would batter in vain. In the southern lands of which the legends spoke, his people might find refuge at last.

It took weeks to discover a pass through which the tribe and the animals could travel. When midsummer came, they had camped in a lonely valley where the air was thin and the stars shone with a brilliance no one had ever seen before.

The summer was waning when Shann took his two sons and went ahead to explore the way. For three days they climbed, and for three nights they slept as best they could on the freezing rocks, and on the fourth morning there was nothing ahead but a gentle rise to a cairn of grey stones built by other travellers, centuries ago.

Shann felt himself trembling, and not with cold, as they walked towards the little pryamid of stones. His sons had fallen behind. No one spoke, for too much was at stake. In a little while they would know if all their hopes had been betrayed.

To east and west, the wall of mountains curved away as if embracing the land beneath. Below lay endless miles of undulating plain, with a great river swinging across it in tremendous loops. It was a fertile land; one in which the tribe could raise crops knowing that there would be no need to flee before the harvest.

Then Shann lifted his eyes to the south, and saw the doom of all his hopes. For there at the edge of the world glimmered that deadly light he had seen so often to the north – the glint of ice below the horizon.

There was no way forward. Through all the years of flight, the glaciers from the south had been advancing to meet them. Soon they would be crushed beneath the moving walls of ice . . .

Southern glaciers did not reach the mountains until a generation later. In that last summer the sons of Shann carried the sacred treasures of the tribe to the lonely cairn overlooking the plain. The ice that had once gleamed below the horizon was now almost at their feet. By spring it would be splintering against the mountain walls.

No one understood the treasures now. They were from a past too distant for the understanding of any man alive. Their origins were lost in the mists that surrounded the Golden Age, and how they had come at last into the possession of this wandering tribe was a story that now would never be told. For it was the story of a civilization that had passed beyond recall.

Once, all these pitiful relics had been treasured for some good reason, and now they had become sacred though their meaning had long been lost. The print in the old books had faded centuries ago though much of the lettering was still visible – if there had been any to read it. But many generations had passed since anyone had had a use for a set of seven-figure logarithms, an atlas of the world, and the score of Sibelius's Seventh Symphony printed, according to the flyleaf, by H. K. Chu and Sons, at the City of Pekin in the year 2371 AD.

The old books were placed reverently in the little crypt that had been made to receive them. There followed a motley collection of fragments – gold and platinum coins, a broken telephoto lens, a watch, a coldlight lamp, a microphone, the cutter from an electric razor, some midget radio tubes, the flotsam that had been left behind when the great tide of civilization had ebbed forever.

All these treasures were carefully stowed away in their resting place. Then came three more relics, the most sacred of all because the least understood.

The first was a strangely shaped piece of metal, showing the colouration of intense heat. It was, in its way, the most pathetic of all these symbols from the past, for it told of man's greatest achievement and of the future he might have known. The mahogany stand on which it was mounted bore a silver plate with the inscription:

Auxiliary Igniter from Starboard Jet
Spaceship 'Morning Star'
Earth-Moon, AD 1985

Next followed another miracle of the ancient science – a sphere of transparent plastic with strangely shaped pieces of metal imbedded in it. At its centre was a tiny capsule of synthetic radio-element, surrounded by the converting screens that shifted its radiation far down the spectrum. As long as the material remained active, the sphere would be a tiny radio transmitter, broadcasting power in all directions. Only a few of these spheres had ever been made. They had been designed as perpetual beacons to mark the orbits of the asteroids. But man had never reached the asteroids and the beacons had never been used.

Last of all was a flat, circular tin, wide in comparison with its depth. It was heavily sealed, and rattled when shaken. The tribal lore predicted that disaster would follow if it were ever opened, and no one knew that it held one of the great works of art of nearly a thousand years before.

The work was finished. The two men rolled the stones back into place and slowly began to descend the mountainside. Even to the last, man had given some thought to the future and had tried to preserve something for posterity.

That winter the great waves of ice began their first assault on the mountains, attacking from north and south. The foothills were overwhelmed in the first onslaught, and the glaciers ground them into dust. But the mountains stood firm, and when the summer came the ice retreated for a while.

So, winter after winter, the battle continued, and the roar of the avalanches, the grinding of rock and the explosions of splintering ice filled the air with tumult. No war of man's had been fiercer than this, and even man's battles had not quite engulfed the globe as this had done.

At last the tidal waves of ice began to subside and to creep slowly down the flanks of the mountains they had never quite subdued. The valleys and passes were still firmly in their grip. It was stalemate. The glaciers had met their match, but their defeat was too late to be of any use to man.

So the centuries passed, and presently there happened something that must occur once at least in the history of every world in the universe, no matter how remote and lonely it may be.

The ship from Venus came five thousand years too late, but its crew knew nothing of this. While still many millions of miles away, the telescopes had seen the great shroud of ice that made Earth the most brilliant object in the sky next to the sun itself.

Here and there the dazzling sheet was marred by black specks that revealed the presence of almost buried mountains. That was all. The rolling oceans, the plains and forests, the deserts and lakes – all that had been the world of man was sealed beneath the ice, perhaps forever.

The ship closed in to Earth and established an orbit less than a thousand miles away. For five days it circled the planet, while cameras recorded all that was left to see and a hundred instruments gathered information that would give the Venusian scientists many years of work.

An actual landing was not intended. There seemed little purpose in it. But on the sixth day the picture changed. A panoramic monitor, driven to the limit of its amplification, detected the dying radiation of the five-thousand-year-old beacon. Through all the centuries, it had been sending out its signals with everfailing strength as its radioactive heart steadily weakened.

The monitor locked on the beacon frequency. In the control room, a bell clamoured for attention. A little later, the Venusian ship broke free from its orbit and slanted down towards Earth, towards a range of mountains that still towered proudly above the ice, and to a cairn of grey stones that the years had scarcely touched . . .

The great disc of the sun blazed fiercely in a sky no longer veiled with mist, for the clouds that had once hidden Venus had now completely gone. Whatever force had caused the change in the sun's radiation had doomed one civilization, but had given birth to another. Less than five thousand years before, the half-savage people of Venus had seen the sun and stars for the first time. Just as the science of Earth had begun with astronomy, so had that of Venus, and on the warm, rich world that man had never seen progress had been incredibly rapid.

Perhaps the Venusians had been lucky. They never knew the Dark Age which had held man enchained for a thousand years. They missed the long detour into chemistry and mechanics but came at once to the more fundamental laws of radiation physics. In the time that man had taken to progress from the Pyramids to the rocket-propelled spaceship, the Venusians had passed from the discovery of agriculture to antigravity itself – the ultimate secret that man had never learned.

The warm ocean that still bore most of the young planet's life rolled its breakers languidly against the sandy shore. So new was this continent that the very sands were coarse and gritty. There had not yet been time enough for the sea to wear them smooth.

The scientists lay half in the water, their beautiful reptilian bodies gleaming in the sunlight. The greatest minds of Venus had gathered on this shore from all the islands of the planet. What they were going to hear they did not know, except that it concerned the Third World and the mysterious race that had peopled it before the coming of the ice.

The Historian was standing on the land, for the instruments he wished to use had no love of water. By his side was a large machine which attracted many curious glances from his colleagues. It was clearly concerned with optics, for a lens system projected from it towards a screen of white material a dozen yards away.

The Historian began to speak. Briefly he recapitulated what little had been discovered concerning the Third Planet and its people.

He mentioned the centuries of fruitless research that had failed to interpret a single word of the writings of Earth. The planet had been inhabited by a race of great technical ability. That, at least, was proved by the few pieces of machinery that had been found in the cairn upon the mountain.

'We do not know why so advanced a civilization came to an end,' he observed. 'Almost certainly, it had sufficient knowledge to survive the Ice Age. There must have been some other factor of which we know nothing. Possibly disease or racial degeneration may have been responsible. It has been suggested that the tribal conflicts endemic to our own species in prehistoric times may have continued on the Third Planet after the coming of technology.

'Some philosophers maintain that knowledge of machinery does not necessarily imply a high degree of civilization, and it is theoretically possible to have wars in a society possessing mechanical power, flight, and even radio. Such a conception is alien to our thoughts, but we must admit its possibility. It would certainly account for the downfall of the lost race.

'It has always been assumed that we should never know anything of the physical form of the creatures who lived on Planet Three. For centuries our artists have been depicting scenes from the history of the dead world, peopling it with all manner of fantastic beings. Most of these creations have resembled us more or less closely, though it has often been pointed out that because *we* are reptiles it does not follow that all intelligent life must necessarily be reptilian.

'We now know the answer to one of the most baffling problems of history. At last, after hundreds of years of research, we have discovered the exact form and nature of the ruling life on the Third Planet.'

There was a murmur of astonishment from the assembled scientists. Some were so taken aback that they disappeared for a while into the comfort of the ocean, as all Venusians were apt to do in moments of stress. The Historian waited until his colleagues re-emerged into the element they so disliked. He himself was quite comfortable, thanks to the tiny sprays that were continually playing over his body. With their help he could live on land for many hours before having to return to the ocean.

The excitement slowly subsided and the lecturer continued, 'One of the most puzzling of the objects found on Planet Three was a flat metal container holding a great length of transparent plastic material, perforated at the edges and wound tightly into a spool. This transparent tape at first seemed quite featureless, but an examination with the new subelectronic microscope has shown that this is not the case. Along the surface material, invisible to our eyes but perfectly clear under the correct radiation, are literally thousands of tiny pictures. It is believed they were imprinted on the material by some chemical means, and have faded with the passage of time.

'These pictures apparently form a record of life as it was on the Third Planet at the height of its civilization. They are not independent. Consecutive pictures are almost identical, differing only in the detail of movement. The purpose of such a record is obvious. It is only necessary to project the scenes in rapid succession to give an illusion of continuous movement. We have made a machine to do this, and I have here an exact reproduction of the picture sequence.

'The scenes you are now going to witness take us

back many thousands of years, to the great days of our sister planet. They show a complex civilization, many of whose activities we can only dimly understand. Life seems to have been very violent and energetic, and much that you will see is quite baffling.

'It is clear that the Third Planet was inhabited by a number of different species, none of them reptilian. That is a blow to our pride, but the conclusion is inescapable. The dominant type of life appears to have been a two-armed biped. It walked upright and covered its body with some flexible material, possibly for protection against the cold, since even before the Ice Age the planet was at a much lower temperature than our own world. But I will not try your patience any further. You will now see the record of which I have been speaking.'

A brilliant light flashed from the projector. There was a gentle whirring, and on the screen appeared hundreds of strange beings moving rather jerkily to and fro. The picture expanded to embrace one of the creatures, and the scientists could see that the Historian's descriptions had been correct.

The creature possessed two eyes, set rather close together, but the other facial adornments were a little obscure. There was a large orifice in the lower portion of the head that was continually opening and closing. Possibly it had something to do with the creature's breathing.

The scientists watched spellbound as the strange being became involved in a series of fantastic adventures. There was an incredibly violent conflict with another, slightly different creature. It seemed certain that they must both be killed, but when it was all over neither seemed any the worse.

Then came a furious drive over miles of country in a four-wheeled mechanical device which was capable of extraordinary feats of locomotion. The ride ended in a city packed with other vehicles moving in all directions at breathtaking speeds. No one was surprised to see two of the machines meet head-on with devastating results.

After that, events became even more complicated. It was now quite obvious that it would take many years of research to analyse and understand all that was happening. It was also clear that the record was a work of art, somewhat stylized, rather than an exact reproduction of life as it actually had been on the Third Planet.

Most of the scientists felt themselves completely dazed when the sequence of pictures came to an end. There was a final flurry of motion, in which the creature that had been the centre of interest became involved in some tremendous but incomprehensible catastrophe. The picture contracted to a circle, centred on the creature's head.

The last scene of all was an expanded view of its face, obviously expressing some powerful emotion. But whether it was rage, grief, defiance, resignation or some other feeling could not be guessed. The picture vanished. For a moment some lettering appeared on the screen, then it was all over.

For several minutes there was complete silence, save for the lapping of the waves upon the sand. The scientists were too stunned to speak. The fleeting glimpse of Earth's civilization had had a shattering effect on their minds. Then little groups began to start talking together, first in whispers and then more and more loudly as the implications of what they had seen became clearer. Presently the Historian called for attention and addressed the meeting again.

'We are now planning,' he said, 'a vast programme of research to extract all available knowledge from this record. Thousands of copies are being made for distribution to all workers. You will appreciate the problem involved. The psychologists in particular have an immense task confronting them.

'But I do not doubt that we shall succeed. In another generation, who can say what we may not have learned of this wonderful race? Before we leave, let us look again at our remote cousins, whose wisdom may have surpassed our own but of whom so little has survived.'

Once more the final picture flashed on the screen, motionless this time, for the projector had been stopped. With something like awe, the scientists gazed at the still figure from the past, while in turn the little biped stared back at them with its characteristic expression of arrogant bad temper.

For the rest of time it would symbolize the human race. The psychologists of Venus would analyse its actions and watch its every movement until they could reconstruct its mind. Thousands of books would be written about it. Intricate philosophies would be contrived to account for its behaviour.

But all this labour, all this research, would be utterly in vain. Perhaps the proud and lonely figure on the screen was smiling sardonically at the scientists who were starting on their age-long fruitless quest.

Its secret would be safe as long as the universe endured, for no one now would ever read the lost language of Earth. Millions of times in the ages to come those last few words would flash across the screen, and none could ever guess their meaning:

A Walt Disney Production.

The Pits Beneath the World

MARY GENTLE

A wind stirs the blue grass of the Great Plains. The flat land stretches out to the perfect circle of the horizon. There is not a rock or tree to break the monotony. Seventeen moons burn in a lilac sky. A blue-giant sun is setting, its white dwarf companion star hangs in the evening sky.

The small figure stands waist-deep in the grass. She aches from running bent over in a crouch. Now she straightens, biting back a gasp at the pain.

Shrill chittering and whistling noises come from the distance. Seen!

Up until today she's been sorry that she's small for her age. Now she's glad. Only a small human could lie concealed in the Plains grass. She edges away and crawls on, hands and knees stained blue by the grass sap.

Behind her, the whistling of the Talinorian hunting party begins again.

There is no doubt: she is their quarry.

When did it go wrong? Pel Graham wondered. The Talinorians are our friends. What happened?

She was hurt and bewildered as well as afraid.

It had all been fine until two days ago . . .

There! – the Talinorian whistled. – The *chelanthi*! –

Pel peered ahead between its sheaf of stalked eyes.

Far out across the Great Plain, grass rippled where no wind blew.

'Hold on!' called Pel's mother, riding high astride the glittering carapace of another Talinorian, Baltenezeril-lashamara.

With a clatter of shell the Talinorian hunting party edged down the side of the cliff. Pel clung as Dalasurieth-rissanihil lurched under her, body-suckers clutching the rock as they moved down the almost vertical surface. The long segmented body rippled.

'Faster!' she yelled, and then remembering that the human voice had too low a frequency for the Talinorian's sensors, tapped the message out on the alien's eye-carapace. The stalked eyes retreated briefly under the hard shell. Pel had learned to interpret this as amusement.

Now they went more slowly. The Talinorians were better suited to rocky cliffs and scarps. Only for the traditional *chelanthi* hunts did they venture down onto grassland.

Pel waved to her mother, and to the other members of the Earth scientific expedition honoured to ride in the Talinorian hunt. It was a time of relaxation. They must have finished negotiating, Pel thought, not very interested. She didn't want to leave Talinor yet.

The wind blew her hair in her eyes. She turned her head, seeing the rocky 'coast' behind them. Clusters of rock rose starkly out of the flat grassland. It was impossible to think of them as anything but islands, jutting out of a grass ocean. On the rocking-gaited Talinorian, Pel felt like a ship at sea. Hunting the beasts of the ocean, the *chelanthi*.

– We're falling behind –

The other unburdened Talinorians were faster. Dalasurieth-rissanihil slowed still further.

The 'islands' they had left were small, and in a

natural condition. They were covered with bush-berry-trees, the purple fruit hanging down in long strings; and with the *cureuk* flowers that folded up when touched. Mothbirds flew only in this hour between the blue sun's rising and the white sun's following, when they again roosted. A multitude of singing insects nested in the crevices of the rock, and the nights were bright with luminous starflies. It was different from Talinor-Prime, Pel thought, where the expedition had set down the shuttle.

– They have made a kill –

–Where? –

Pel stared ahead over Dalasurieth-rissanihil's carapace, but saw nothing in detail. If she admitted the truth she preferred riding to hunting, and wasn't sorry to miss the end.

A wisp of smoke coiled up ahead.

– Dala', look! –

– Stray laser-beam. Don't they realize what a grass fire might do? –

Dalasurieth-rissanihil sounded, so far as she could tell, furious.

– I thought you had to use spears? –

– Tradition demands it. The leader will have something to say to them back at Prime! –

Pel saw the Talinorians put the fire out before it could spread. Others carried the scaly *chelanthi* slung across their patterned carapaces, held in place by their forked scorpion-tails. Clusters of thin jointed arms waved excitedly.

– Will you stay for the hunt tomorrow? –

– I have to go home. It's my . . . – The click and whistle language failed her. – It's a party. The northern team should be back. And besides, it's my . . . –

She couldn't find a word for 'birthday', and struggled to make it clear. Dalasurieth-rissanihil rattled its forked tail.

– So you will have been alive eleven seasons of your home world? That is a long time to be adult. I had thought you younger –

Privately she laughed. Aliens were often stupid about the most obvious things. Except, she thought, I don't suppose it *is* obvious to them; not even an eleventh birthday . . .

– How old are you, Dala'? –

– I have been adult three seasons –

Pel couldn't be bothered to translate that into Earth-standard years. She knew it wasn't long.

– Yes, but how long ago were you born? I mean, I'm not adult. Not exactly. I don't come of age until I'm fourteen –

– You are not adult? –

– No, not yet; I told you. Oh, you don't understand –

They were turning back towards the islands and Talinor-Prime. Dalasurieth-rissanihil was unusually silent on the way back across the plain, and she wondered if she had offended him.

Talinor-Prime. An 'island' in a grassland 'ocean', but this island was a continent. Big enough to take a flyer three days to cross it. A rock plateau a few metres higher than the surrounding plain, and with a totally different ecology – as Pel's xenobiologist mother was very prone to telling her. More important from Pel's point of view, Talinor-Prime held the city and the starship landing-field.

It was noon before they arrived. The two suns – blue Alpha and white Beta – blazed together in the sky. Pel had a black and a purple shadow following her on the carved rock walkway.

'Ready for the party tomorrow?' her mother asked.

'You bet. Are the others back yet?'

'Not yet. I'm expecting them to call in soon.'

The long arthropod bodies of the Talinorians glided past them on low trollies. Some preferred the powered walkways that riddled the rock of Prime. They were too low for an adult human to enter without stooping, but Pel was small enough to stand upright in them.

They turned down another walkway and saw the starfield between the wasp-nest dwellings of the Talinorians. Pel looked through the view-grills as they walked. She liked the inside of the 'nests', with their powered valve-doors and beam-operated equipment. Talinorian manipulative limbs weren't strong, but they were good at delicate work. Their great love was glass, which their formulae made stronger than anywhere else in the galaxy. Sculptured, woven in filaments, blown into spheres and cubes and octagons, the ornaments glittered in the light of the two suns; and Talinor-Prime chimed as the wind blew.

'Pel!'

Pel ran on from staring through a view-grill. She caught up as they began to walk across the vast expanse of the starfield. The blue-grey rock was hot underfoot.

'Tell me,' her mother said, 'what do you and Dala' talk about?'

'Oh . . . things.' Pel shrugged.

'I'm sorry in a way that there are no other kids with this expedition. I always wonder if it's fair to bring you on these trips. But since there are just the two of us . . .'

Pel made a rude noise. 'Try and stop me coming with you,' she invited. 'Anyway, it's training – for the future.'

Her mother laughed.

The starfield was on a long spit of 'island' jutting out into the grassland. At that time there were no other ships there. Pel looked at the squat dirty shuttle with affection. It would be great to have the other half of the team back with the ship.

I wonder if they brought me any presents? she thought; and didn't answer when her mother asked her what she was grinning at.

Blue Alpha's dawn light stretched her shadow far behind her on the rocks. The morning smelled clean, spicy. A cool wind blew out of the south. Pel scrambled down the long spit towards the edge of the grassland. Mothbirds beat their fragile wings round her, bright against the amethyst sky.

She could just have waited on the shuttle. But Pel preferred to keep watch in the open, and wait for the ship's return.

Something whirred past her ear.

She swatted at it automatically. Glancing round, she saw some Talinorians on the slope above her, and recognized one of them as Dalasurieth-rissanihil.

A shadow flicked her face.

The spear clattered on the rock beside her.

Pel sprang up. The red line of a laser kicked the rock into molten steam. While she watched, Dalasurieth-rissanihil raised the gun and took aim again.

She took a flying leap off the rocks, running as fast as she could through the grass. It slowed her, but she managed to reach the cover of a rock overhang.

Another party of Talinorians waited beyond it.

She swerved out into the open, running like a hare. Arms and legs pumping, lungs burning; she fell into a stride that took her far out into the blue grassland.

It dawned on her as she fell into the scant cover that the grass afforded, far from Talinor-Prime, that those first shots had not been meant to kill. Only to start her running. Only to force her out into the grass ocean, where killing might take place honourably with glass-tipped hunting spears.

She put her head down, gripped her knees, and tried to stop shaking. When the first panic subsided, bewilderment remained. Then it hardened into a cold determination.

Pel Graham looked back to the distant cliffs of Prime. She thought, Somehow I'll get back. I'll make them pay. Somehow I'll find out . . . Dalasurieth-rissanihil – *why*?

She heard the hunting party in the distance.

Evening found her still further away, driven out of sight of Prime. The islands were specks on the horizon. If it had not been for the gentle ridges and undulations of the ground here, she would have been spotted long ago. Now she clung to cover under an alien sky. The grassland went from aquamarine to azure to indigo as Beta set.

The expedition will come looking, Pel thought. I only have to stay free until the shuttle flies over and finds me. I bet they're already on their way –

The grass rustled.

Pel flopped down on her stomach. A blunt muzzle pushed through the reed-bladed grass. A *chelanthi*. Its low flexible body was covered in mirror-scales, camouflaging it. She saw tiny eye-clusters almost hidden under the muzzle. The actual mouth was further back, between the front pair of legs. As she watched, it began to crop the grass.

Aren't they meat-eaters? Pel wondered.

A scaly hide brushed her arm. She shot back, biting off a yell. The *chelanthi* raised its muzzle, eye-stalks wavering reproachfully. Pel stifled laughter. It scuttled off past the first *chelanthi*. She followed it.

The ridge concealed a dip beyond. The hollow was pitted with holes, among which many *chelanthi* were grazing. They seemed harmless. They probably were . . .

Another *chelanthi* emerged from one of the pits. They must burrow deep, Pel thought. How else would they hide from the Talinorians?

A long whistle sounded through the gathering twilight. She thought, what if the hunters have heat-seeking equipment? That'll show up human body-heat miles off when it's dark . . .

Pel Graham grinned. It was a crazy idea she had. Good, but crazy; still, she might be a little crazy herself by now. There was every excuse for it.

The *chelanthi* did not object when Pel crept into one of the pits beside them. It was dry, earth trodden down hard, and surprisingly roomy. She lay sheltered among their warm scaly bodies, hidden from anything on the grassland above.

The blue sun set in an ocean-coloured sky. The few stars of the galaxy's rim burned in lonely splendour. The moons rose, all seventeen of Talinor's satellites. Sometimes their varying orbits made them appear in clusters, but now they hung in a string of crescents. Pel Graham slept fitfully in the warm night. The Talinorian hunting party passed five miles to the west.

Morning came chill. Disturbed out of one pit when the *chelanthi* went to graze, Pel crawled into another. It had only one occupant. This *chelanthi* made a racheting noise like a broken clock and nipped at her hand. Pel backed out in an undignified scramble.

She watched. The *chelanthi* was busy at the mouth of that pit. It appeared to be stringing a substance from glands under its body. The stubby forepaws gripped the pit's mouth, and Pel saw that it was beginning to weave a web over it.

She listened, but heard no sound of the hunt.

I'm safe here. At least I'm hidden. But I have to get back to Prime. I have to warn them!

The day wore on. Pel was extremely bored by the *chelanthi*. True, they did her no harm. They did nothing except crop the grass. The webbed pit remained closed, and she was not sure if the *chelanthi* inside were sleeping, hibernating, or dead. Hourly the mass of its hidden body became more shapeless.

Unless the Talinorians stumbled across her, the *chelanthi* would hide her. They camouflaged her against long-distance night sensors, and in the day radiation from the two suns made long-distance sensing impossible.

It was not until then that it occurred to her; if she was hidden from Talinorian sensors, she must also be hidden from those of the Earth expedition.

The second evening came. The blue giant Alpha eclipsed the white dwarf Beta as the suns set. Pel was hungrier than she had ever thought it possible to be. Thirst made her drink the water that collected on the flat-bladed grass, and hope that it didn't carry infection.

She was even more determined to get back to Talinor-Prime. It was think of that, or panic, and she didn't dare panic.

The *chelanthi* gave up grazing and headed for the pits.

Pel thought about the webbed pit, she hadn't looked at it in a while. She walked over to it.

As she watched, the webbing over the pit's entrance twitched. It bulged as if something beneath it were trying to get out. Pel stepped back rapidly.

The webbing reared up and split. Something sharp, grey, and glistening protruded. It twitched again, slitting the web still further. A multitude of thin many-jointed and hard-shelled limbs followed, gripping the sides of the pit. A carapace emerged. Under it, clustered eye-stalks waved. The body heaved itself up onto the grass, segment by armoured segment, disclosing the suckers on the underside. The patterned shell gleamed. Last to leave the pit was the forked scorpion-tail.

Pel stared.

The young Talinorian looked round at the grass-eating *chelanthi*, at Pel Graham who stood frozen with astonishment, and clicked and whistled softly. As it scuttled off it said – Don't you know that there are some things it's better for you not to see? –

It changes everything! Pel thought.

The grass was harsh under her hands and knees. She followed the line of a low ridge. The pits and the broken web were far behind her. She knew that the new-born Talinorian would betray her to the hunting party as soon as it found them.

White Beta rose, and the plains flooded with colour. A little warmth came back to Pel as she moved.

It spoke. It was a *chelanthi*, and it – changed.

It had looked very like Dalasurieth-rissanihil, who was only three seasons 'adult'.

Shrilly in the distance came the whistle of the hunters. Abandoning the *chelanthi*, she had abandoned safety.

I will get back to Prime! she told herself.

She saw something flash in the morning sky like a thrown coin.

'Hey! Hey, shuttle!'

They'll never hear me, never see me, never sense me . . . If there was any way I could mark myself out . . .

Fire would have been best, but she had no way to set the grass lands on fire. And then she remembered the *chelanthi* hunt.

Deliberately Pel stood up and ran to the crown of the ridge. She waved both arms over her head, semaphoring wildly.

The shrilling of the hunters was louder, much louder.

As fleet as fear could make her, she ran. A laser-beam licked redly out to her left, and even through her exhaustion she had time for a grin of triumph.

A line of grass burst into crackling fire. The shuttle's course veered widly. It began to descend.

Pel could hardly breathe. The world was going red and black round her. But she staggered over the ramp a hundred yards ahead of her pursuers and fell into her mother's arms.

The Talinorian hunting party dwindled below.

'*That* took some sorting out. You mustn't blame them,' Pel's mother turned away from the computer console. 'It's not uncommon in nature to have a larval stage, after all. Even on Earth, moths and butterflies . . . And until they change they're quite unintelligent. Just animals, really.'

'Did you tell them?' Pel asked. 'About – children?'

Outside the shuttle's viewpoint, Talinor-Prime sparkled in the light of two suns. The wind ruffled the grasslands.

'It's a great step forward in understanding each other.' She put her hand on Pel's shoulder. 'You see, when you said you weren't adult –'

'They thought it was all right to hunt me down?'

'Don't be bitter. Worlds are different places.' She turned her back. 'If they'd hurt *you* . . .'

Pel knew what that note in her mother's voice meant. Lightly she said, 'I'm all right.'

'I know you are, love.'

But you don't understand, she thought. Dalasur-ieth-rissanihil was my friend . . .

'Were you afraid? Oh, that's a stupid question . . . it was a brave thing you did, Pel.'

'Will they stop the hunting?'

'You don't have to be afraid. Not now it's been made clear to everyone.'

'No.' Pel shook her head impatiently. 'The *chelanthi* hunting. Will you stop that?'

'You know we can't interfere on alien worlds.' Her mother sat down at the console. 'You get some rest. I'm going to pilot us in.'

The door irised shut. Back in the main body of the shuttle, Pel stared out of the port. Hunger, exhaustion; she has been told that these will pass.

Two suns cast the descending shuttle's double shadow on the landing-field. She remembers the endless grassland like a great sea. She remembers Talinor-Prime jutting up in headlands and cliffs and peaks. And she remembers the pits beneath the world, and the *chelanthi* as they nuzzled at her in their sleep.

She sits down and hides her face in her hands.

Pel Graham is thinking of the other children.